Finding the Words:
Talking Children through the Tough Times

Rosaleen McElvaney is a lecturer in psychotherapy in Dublin City University. She is a clinical psychologist with many years' experience working in the public health services in Ireland. Her PhD thesis was on the topic of child sexual abuse.

Finding the Words

Talking Children through the Tough Times

Rosaleen McElvaney

VERITAS

Published 2015 by
Veritas Publications
7–8 Lower Abbey Street
Dublin 1, Ireland
publications@veritas.ie
www.veritas.ie

ISBN 978 1 84730 595 4
Copyright © Rosaleen McElvaney, 2015

10 9 8 7 6 5 4 3 2 1

A catalogue record for this book is available from the British Library.

Cover designed by Barbara Croatto, Veritas
Printed in the Republic of Ireland by Watermans Printers Ltd, Cork

Veritas books are printed on paper made from the wood pulp of managed forests. For every tree felled, at least one tree is planted, thereby renewing natural resources.

My list of thanks yous!

To the many children and parents who I have met through my work: for sharing your stories and teaching me about talking with children.

To Donna, my commissioning editor: for the idea for this book and for the gentle and firm guidance throughout; and to Daragh, the managing editor at Veritas, for bringing me through the final hoops.

To my big sister, Tricia: for the constant encouragement and reassurance that I knew more than I thought I did.

To Carmel, Audrey & Abigail: for your helpful feedback.

To my husband, Frank: for your patience and support, always there when needed.

To my children, Lorcan and Fergus, who although now on the cusp of adulthood, will always be 'my children': for teaching me how to be a parent, when to talk and when to listen.

Contents

Introduction

Over the years, working as a clinical psychologist, I have been asked many times: How would I talk to the kids about that? Often the question would come from a concerned parent who feels uncomfortable with the topic that they want to bring up with their son or daughter. This sense of uneasiness can create a major barrier in talking with children about sensitive topics.

If we are not comfortable about talking ourselves, how can we hope to talk with our children? Often our concern is that the topic will be upsetting – how, for instance, do we tell very young family members that their grandparent has just past away? Or that a beloved pet has to be put down?

What should we tell them? How much should we tell them? When is the best time to tell them? Should we leave it until the last minute so they have less time to worry about it or should we tell them ahead of time so that they have time to absorb it, time to talk about how they feel? It probably will be upsetting for our children to talk about difficult things. These are upsetting realities. But children face upsetting realities every day. For the most part they are better able to cope than we give them credit for.

This book is about having conversations with children about the hard things in life. Many of us may have grown up in families where such subjects were not talked about. We want to do better by our children and to foster open communication with them. We do this in the hope that one day, if our child is upset about something, they will come to us and talk to us openly. We know that we can't read our children's minds (even if sometimes we let them think that we can!). We know that we have to rely to a great extent on them coming to us to talk about things if they need to. So we want to set a good example early in their lives. We want to be the parent who can have these kinds of conversations with our children.

Reflecting on our own discomfort is the first step. Preparing ourselves for the conversation is important. We need to think through how we feel about the issue in question. Then we need to think about how our own feelings are likely to affect how we talk about it and how we respond to what our child may say about it. If we are going to get upset, then perhaps this is not the time to talk about it. Or perhaps we should delegate the task to someone else, someone who will not feel compromised by his or her emotions.

Just as we are concerned about upsetting our children, so too our children are often concerned about upsetting us. Children, for the most part, are extremely protective of their parents, particularly their mothers. They depend on us and so they need us to be strong for them. If we are upset, who can they rely on? They are also highly perceptive. We may be expert at hiding our feelings from our friends, and even our partners, but hiding emotions from our children is a bit more difficult. As we get older we learn to manage our moods and decide when it's best to show others how we feel and when it's not. Sometimes, in order to protect others from hurt, we learn how to suppress difficult emotions. Many children have not yet learned to manage their feelings. But just as young children can be like an open book, they can also see through us and are very sensitive to our feelings and reactions.

Chapter One examines the importance of self awareness – being aware of our own feelings and thoughts and the role this plays in parenting and in how we talk with our children. Many of us deal with difficult experiences by trying to forget about them, and getting on with our lives. This works well for some kinds of difficulties, mostly the minor ones. For more challenging experiences, such as growing up in a family where one or both parents were verbally or physically abusive, moving on often requires prolonged periods of reflection. In order to move forward, we often have to spend a considerable amount of time confronting what happened, thus allowing ourselves to 'process' emotions that we may have long suppressed.

If we don't understand how our own childhood experiences have affected us – for good and for ill – there is a danger that our own 'issues' will prevent us from being able to help our children when they run into trouble. We may see our difficulties reflected in theirs and assume that their experience is the same as ours, just because there may be some superficial similarities. We may impose our views on them without even realising it. This will not only undermine our responsibility as parents, it can harm our children who are vulnerable and so easily influenced by us.

Reflecting on our childhood allows us to process the experience, to 'deal with it' in a way that is emotionally healthy. Bringing these sometimes painful experiences out into the open and pondering their impact on our lives is the healthiest way to cope with them. Then we can truly move on. In chapter one, I talk about the importance of taking time to reflect on ourselves and how this can help us to be there for our children. By doing so, we are better able to allow our children to be themselves, to have their own feelings about formative life experiences, while also learning to help them cope with difficult events that will inevitably come their way.

We have to be aware of what is 'our stuff' and what is 'their stuff' if we are to support them through difficult times. Chapter One will, I hope, help readers learn how to separate the two. Much of what we learn about what works in counselling and psychotherapy comes from our understanding of good parenting, or 'good enough' parenting, as the psychologist Bruno Bettelheim refers to it in his book *A Good Enough Parent*.[1] Bettelheim recognised, as did many others in the field of psychology and psychotherapy, that it is not about being the perfect parent, it is about being good enough.

Chapter Two examines how communication styles may change throughout childhood and adolescence. Communication is a two-way process – giving and receiving. It involves the person who is trying to communicate and the person who is trying to understand. It is also reciprocal in that as we communicate with another person we are influenced by their reactions to us as we engage in this conversation. I also discuss how communication encompasses more than simply words. Younger children are much more in touch with their whole person – body, mind and soul. Therefore they communicate as a whole being. Adults tend to be very focused on the language children use. Overreliance on the words children deploy can lead to misunderstandings and miscommunications. Older children rely more on language but also reflect more on what they say and are more conscious and aware of how people may react to their words. They are better at hiding their feelings. In this chapter, I describe how children's sense of understanding changes as they get older, how we, as parents, communicate differently with children and young people of different ages and how they communicate differently with us.

Chapter Three and **Chapter Four** deal with ways of talking with children about separation and death. While I refer in these chapters to parents separating, it is important to note that similar issues apply to many forms of separation, be it moving house, moving school or moving away from friends. Talking with children about change, particularly if it is a difficult transition, brings up similar feelings.

Each change brings loss as well as potential gains. However, sometimes we are so focused on the positive facets of change that

---

1   Bruno Bettelheim, *A Good Enough Parent: A Book on Child Rearing*, (New York: Alfred A. Knapf, 1987).

we neglect to appreciate the attendant losses. Change brings the unfamiliar. For many children this can be exciting but for many others the loss of the familiar is more keenly felt.

Dealing with loss and adapting to change are key developmental tasks that face all of us as we go through life. This can be very challenging for parents who are worried about how their children will react to these conversations. I will refer to how children of varying ages may require different kinds of conversations about these issues but I always emphasise the variation among individual children. One four-year-old child might have more in common with the average seven-year-old child than with peers of the same age. Children's personalities are just as important as their different developmental stages in terms of how they talk with us about difficult feelings and worries they may have.

Chapter Five concerns talking with children about bullying. Most children will come into contact with the issue of bullying at some stage during their childhood or adolescence, whether by being a victim, a perpetrator or simply through observing bullying incidents. Talking with them from an early age about bullying and how to deal with incidents if they arise can protect our children and ensure that they come to us if they are experiencing this in their peer group.

Chapter Six covers talking with children about child sexual abuse. We know from large-scale studies that approximately up to one in four children may experience sexual abuse. This covers a wide range of abusive experiences from being intentionally exposed to sexual material, to being raped. Most children are abused by someone they know and in many cases it can gradually develop over time so that the child is unsure as to what's really happening until it is too late. We know that children have difficulty reaching out for help for a number of reasons. Younger children may not understand what's happening, they may not have the words to communicate this experience. Older children understand only too well that this is not okay and they are often afraid of the consequences of speaking out, knowing that it will cause considerable upset in a family; they will often feel responsible for being the ones to have caused this chaos by making themselves heard.

We know that the first step for parents in being able to help their children when they have been abused is to have been informed about it – we therefore depend on our children being able to communicate this to us, in whatever way they can. Given that children can be sexually abused from the time they are babies, it is important to begin to have conversations about sexual abuse from as early as possible in a child's life. The kinds of conversations we have will of course vary according to their age. Chapter six contains some pointers to think about in having these conversations with your child.

Most children, thankfully, will not experience sexual abuse. Nevertheless, many of the suggestions I make here in relation to sexual abuse also relate to bullying or other difficult experiences that children may have. Protecting our children from sexual abuse is about helping them understand their rights and their entitlement to be treated with respect and dignity. It is about helping our children recognise when behaviour is not okay, and to trust their instincts when they feel that something is not right. It is about empowering our children to stand up for themselves, not to tolerate it when others treat them badly, and to come to us for support if they are not able to manage the situation themselves or if, as in the case of sexual abuse, it is a matter for adults to deal with.

Chapter Seven is a little different from the others in that I deal here with children communicating with each other and how we as parents and adults in their lives can support this. Parents know that during the teenage years in particular, our children often look to their friends for emotional support in the first instance, rather than to us directly. Teachers often advise parents to establish and maintain good relationships with fellow parents, as this is a good way of keeping an eye on what's happening in their children's lives.

Young people differ in terms of how much they talk at home about the ups and downs of their daily lives. Some will talk openly to their parents while others will be less communicative. This is not necessarily a reflection on parents. It is often just a consequence of children's differing personalities. Keeping in touch with other parents and highlighting the fact we are doing so to our children often serves as a strong protective factor in helping our adolescent children (and us) navigate through the teenage years.

Chapter Eight examines how we talk with our children when we are really concerned about them and think that professional help is needed. As parents, we want to promote our children's psychological well-being but sometimes we don't have the answers – sometimes we need additional help. The earlier we get this help the better. It is easier to address difficulties in the earlier stages of their development. Getting help early also helps to prevent more serious difficulties from developing.

Parents are often the first to notice that something is not right in their child's world but they can also be the last. Small families nowadays mean that parents do not have the same ability to make comparisons with other children. They may not realise the extent to which their child is different from other children. Or they may see this as reflecting their child's individual personality rather than seeing it as a sign that there is something seriously wrong, and that their child, or they as a family, need help. This chapter will highlight some points to think about when parents are worried that they may need to seek professional help for their children. The chapter will also include some information about the different ways that psychologists and psychotherapists work with children and families. This will hopefully help parents to decide on what might be best for your child and your family.

I have chosen to focus on these key topics in this book because it seems to me that many of the issues they raise are applicable across a range of other areas that parents and children have to deal with. My hope is that you, the reader, will be able to adapt what I've written and apply this to an array of topics or situations.

I have chosen to use the terms 'he' and 'she' interchangeably throughout the book to be inclusive of both genders. There are differences of course between boys and girls. In general, girls reflect more on their emotional lives and talk more about their feelings. But in this book I am concerned more with the particular than the general. Making assumptions about our children on the basis of gender can blind us to their uniqueness. I try to emphasise this throughout the book: children differ, independent of gender. As a parent I am encouraging you to think about you and your particular child. Your son may well be what is regarded as a 'typical boy' in the way he does or doesn't express himself. But how much of that is to do with what we expect of him? How much is it to do with social conditioning? We talk of boys as not being 'as good' at articulating their thoughts and feelings, but how do we measure 'good'? Girls are certainly more verbal and typically have a more advanced vocabulary at an earlier age than boys. In peer conflicts, girls will reflect more and express their hurt more; they will hold onto this hurt for longer and it will typically take longer to resolve than conflicts among boys. But is this better? Or just different? When we talk about wanting boys to express their feelings more – because we believe that it is better for their psychological well-being – what do we mean by 'more'? Is it that we wonder why can't a boy ... be more like a girl?

There are two dangers, in my view, of focusing on gender. First, as previously mentioned, it brings our attention to the general rather than to the particular, to the 'typical child' rather than to our child. While it is useful to be aware of what is typical for boys or girls, it is more important to get to know the individual child. Second, it can lead us to devaluing how our individual child expresses him or herself, if we have expectations of them that are based on what we regard as 'normal' or 'typical'. We need to get to know our individual children and learn how to communicate with them.

ONE

Know Yourself

As parents, we are the most powerful influence on our children, particularly in the early years. That is both exciting and scary. It places a responsibility on us not just to care for our children in terms of feeding, clothing and providing the basics, it also means that both consciously and unconsciously we set an example to them of how to be in ourselves and how to be in the world. While we want to set a good example for them and teach them about life, we also want to give them enough space to grow in themselves, and not to be overshadowed by us.

In this chapter, I will talk about the importance of knowing ourselves and being able to separate out our feelings, thoughts and worries from those of our children's. While we know our children better than anyone, we can get it wrong at times. We can confuse what's best for them with what we think is best for them. As a result of knowing them so well we can sometimes think that we 'know it all', while in fact other people may know them better in some ways than we do. We can assume we know what our children are thinking or feeling when we don't. We can jump to the conclusion that they feel this way because that is how we would feel if we were in their situation. Becoming more aware of our own feelings helps us give our children more space to have their own.

Picture this: a mother and daughter in an embrace in the schoolyard, the first day back at school. One might assume that the child is upset and is clinging to her mother, fearful of her leaving. As they part, it becomes clear that the mother is sobbing while the child is looking at her with concern but doesn't appear to be upset herself. I will use this example to illustrate the different ways that this scene can be interpreted. In doing so, I will highlight how we as parents need to mind ourselves in order to better enable us to mind our children.

There are two key ways to get to know ourselves better: reflecting on ourselves and getting feedback from others. Sometimes parents are good at reflecting on what they see as the mistakes they make – they can brood over this for days, asking questions like should I have said that? Was that the wrong thing to do? It is equally, if not more important, to reflect on the positive things we do and say. Congratulating ourselves on the things we get right is also important – often there is no one else there to notice so we need to do it for ourselves.

Parents can be so busy just getting through the day that they don't have the time or don't take the time to reflect on what's happening in their lives. There can be too much focus on doing it right and not enough on how do I feel about all this? Yet it is our ability to reflect on ourselves, on what makes us tick and on how we feel about things, that enables us to be there for others in a truly caring way.

Taking time out on a daily basis to stop and think: how am I? is crucial for the job of parenting. It is not necessarily the answer to this question that is so important, but the question itself. In the western world we have become so caught up in the way we think about our lives that we have neglected to some extent to think about how we feel in our bodies. Sometimes rather than asking ourselves: what do I think about that? we could ask: what do I feel about that? Am I exhausted? Am I tense and nervous? Where do I feel it in my body? What do I need in order to look after myself right now? Do I need ten minutes to sit and relax? Do I need to get out for a walk? Do I need to chat to a friend? Listening to ourselves more and asking ourselves the question: what do I need right now? is important for our psychological well-being. What's good for us is good for our children; minding ourselves will enable us to be there for them.

The reality is that it is very difficult to stop and think and feel if we are busy all the time. If we are so taken up with the list of things to do each day, it's hard to make time for checking in with ourselves. I'm not talking about a lot of time – for many people, a few minutes here and there does the trick. For others, it's about setting aside a distinct chunk of time. It is about prioritising, just like we do each day with our to-do lists. It's often not possible to get through the whole list each day. We have to decide what's most urgent and what's most important. Some chores will just have to wait. Putting 'me' on that list is a good starting point.

Often when parents are stressed, this is the time they have these conversations about 'me time'. Well-meaning friends may make suggestions as to what they could do to mind themselves better. But how would I get the time to do that? is often the response to a suggestion. It's important to understand that it is not about quantity of time. If you reflect on how time is spent each day, you can make space to do other things – there is time to do the washing, there is time to prepare dinner. It is the way we prioritise our time and our tasks that needs to be addressed. It is about realising and acknowledging that 'me time' is a priority rather than a luxury. Whether that's taking time out in your week to catch up with friends, meditate, exercise or read, it's essential to treat such activities as integral to our lives, rather than optional add-ons.

If these activities are planned deliberately as 'me time' we can appreciate the time more for ourselves, we can benefit more from them and as such will be better able to assist others.

So what are the drawbacks to not taking this 'me time'? Why bother if we're doing just fine? Maybe we're enjoying spending every spare minute of every day with our children and being there exclusively for them. If this is the case, I would encourage you to ask yourself: what am I getting out of this? Do I need to be needed all the time? Does my being there 'on tap' for my children fill a vacuum in my life? Do I feel better about myself through being there for my children? Is this the source of my self-esteem?

If the answers to some of these questions are 'yes' then more reflection is needed. What happens when our babies and toddlers don't need us so much? What happens when their instinctive drive towards independence is blossoming and they need to separate or distance themselves from us? What happens when they prefer to spend time with others than with us? What happens when they want to do things for themselves rather than us doing them for them? What then happens to our self-esteem? The danger, of course, is that we will cling onto them, much like the mother in the schoolyard mentioned at the beginning of this chapter. We run the risk of stifling their growing sense of independence in an attempt to have our own needs met. Our needs will take priority over their needs, and we will be failing them as parents.

The second way to know ourselves better is to ask those who know us well for feedback. Sometimes clients say to me: you're the only person in my life who is really honest with me. You say it as it is. I think it is sad that people are not always able to be honest with their loved ones. We are not doing each other any favours by tiptoeing around difficult subjects and avoiding speaking the truth out of fear of causing offence. We can't learn how to be better people if we are not able to face up to the aspects of ourselves that are not entirely pleasant. When we have friends who can be really honest with us, it helps us identify aspects of ourselves that we are blind to – it is natural and human to be blind to our faults. It also deepens friendships when we can be truly honest with each other. A good friend is someone who can kindly, and from a place of genuine concern, take issue with our behaviour. Of course they may not always get it right – but having the conversation will help you reflect on your actions, be they healthy or otherwise. It is a chance to learn more about yourself, what you do, the way you do it and even maybe why you do it.

An interesting therapeutic method used in helping parents is the *Marte Meo* method. Put simply, this involves videotaping parents interacting with their children and working with a therapist using the resulting footage to enhance parenting skills and experiences. When parents look back at these videos they are often surprised at what they see. When we look at ourselves on videotape, it helps us understand ourselves better. It is human to 'not see' our weaknesses, our 'blind spots'. When we see videotaped evidence of how we are, we can no longer remain blind. We can't deny what we are doing – we can't wiggle out of it so easily. The evidence is there. Seeing our own behaviour helps us acknowledge the way we behave. Then we can do something about changing it if need be. So too with friends or partners: getting feedback on how we interact with our children in a caring, non-confrontational manner can help us gain insight into the way we parent.

Of course, the best way of knowing ourselves and how we are as parents is to simply ask our children. We may not like what we hear but they are the best source of information on the topic. We may see ourselves as very different from how they see us. If so, isn't this worth exploring? Why is it that what they see is so different? It may be that they don't have the whole picture. What they focus on is the small picture – how you are today, in this moment, on this issue. For you, this may be part of an overall strategy that you use to try to reinforce a message. But the small picture is important too. Children form their impressions of us from an accumulation of all these small pictures. We want to make sure that all that adds up to the same big picture that we're trying to achieve.

Let's come back to the mother in the schoolyard. Why do we suppose she was so upset? Perhaps she had really enjoyed spending time with her daughter over the summer months and was going to miss her now that she was back at school? Perhaps her daughter was having some worries about going back to school and the mother was feeling these more intensely than her daughter was? In the latter case, perhaps the mother was expressing what the daughter was feeling, just in a different way? Perhaps the mother herself had struggled with separations and the return to school at the end of each summer in her own childhood and her daughter's experience was triggering this memory for her? Perhaps another school year was a reminder that her daughter was getting older and becoming more her own person and this was difficult for the mother?

The important question is: whose distress was being expressed here – the mother's or the daughter's? In the first scenario, the mother is upset at the summer coming to an end and a new term beginning. She has so enjoyed the time spent with her daughter and now they are back to the daily school routine and the separations that entails. In this case, the mother's distress could be difficult for the daughter to manage. The child may feel guilty for going to school and leaving her mother. This can interfere with the girl's ability to engage in new experiences and to enjoy them accordingly.

In extreme cases this may lead to what we call 'school refusal', whereby a child refuses to go to school out of concern for the parent's welfare. Perhaps in this case, there is a duty for this mother to reflect on her own needs and think about how she can get those needs met other than through her daughter. She may need to look for new experiences that will give her a sense of belonging and independence that might be missing from life. She may need to reflect on how her neediness may be impacting on her daughter. There may be incidents she can reflect upon in which her daughter has refused to take advantage of opportunities to be with friends or try new experiences because she stays at home with Mum.

In the second scenario, the daughter may be experiencing some distress at going back to school but it is the mother who is actually expressing the distress in this instance. Perhaps the daughter has been talking to her mother about her worries and it is the daughter's unexpressed distress that her mother is feeling, rather than her own. This mother may be very tuned into her daughter's emotional state and there may be a pattern between the two with the mother 'feeling for' the daughter. Parents of infants will identify with this experience whereby you 'pick up' on the distress of your baby and you feel it intensely. In this instance the feeling is elicited in you by the baby's sense of discomfort. The job of the parent in this case is to 'manage' the 'unmanageable'. The parent might talk to themselves as follows: calm down, okay what could be wrong? Perhaps he's hungry. Perhaps she needs her nappy changed? Perhaps he's tired and needs a nap? Perhaps she has trapped wind?

Thinking through the various possibilities helps the parent calm down, helps them get on top of their feelings, helps them gain control of the situation and take charge. This taking charge in itself helps the parent calm down and in turn helps the baby. However, the urgency of the situation requires that the parent feels the distress that the baby is feeling. It is part of the baby's psychological development that they can communicate their turmoil to the parent or guardian and, in response, have their needs met. In this way, the parent can react accordingly and provide the soothing environment necessary for the baby to thrive. Over time, as the relationship develops and there are multiple interactions such as those described above, the baby develops the ability to self soothe. They know that the parent will 'hear' their distress and will respond. The baby learns to soothe themselves as they wait for their needs to be met by the parent.

As children get older they develop the ability to communicate their discomfort both non-verbally and verbally. The classic non-verbal signs are the so-called 'psychosomatic' complaints such as the tummy ache and the headache. Children are helped to develop a language for communicating their distress, typically from being asked questions by their parents and carers: do you feel sad? Do you feel upset? Do you feel frustrated? Do you feel angry? Some children, however, continue to communicate their pain non-verbally and rely on their parents to 'pick up' on the signs and interpret the communication.

As with the example of the parent and infant, the parent of the older child may 'feel' the child's distress. The child for some reason is unable to tolerate this feeling in herself – it might be too overwhelming for her and so she needs her parent to feel it for her and to be able to respond in this soothing way to help the child manage the feeling herself. In the schoolyard scenario, it may be that the mother was feeling the distress for her daughter but was struggling with managing this anxiety herself. She may need to reflect on how she can learn to contain the anguish for her daughter – to acknowledge it, to name it for her daughter but not to be overwhelmed by it. Unfortunately, if a parent is not able to manage the feelings, the message they are giving their child is: you are right not to feel this. It is unmanageable, look at me: I can't even cope with it. This is not good for the child who needs to develop the ability to regulate her emotions and take charge of how she feels and expresses them.

Beginning school and the return to school at the end of each summer break gives us a good snapshot of how we all deal with separations. It is about how we manage change and transition – are we comfortable enough in ourselves to be able to move into a new environment without pining too much for the comfort zone of the old? Do we experience an overwhelming ache at the loss of the old that gets in the way of our openness to enjoy the new? We all have our own ways of dealing with these transitions and while each new experience builds on the old, we do develop a particular way of coping with change as we go through life. If we feel insecure in ourselves we will probably find new situations more challenging to deal with. Our children learn from us. They watch us every day in how we deal with new situations. They may learn from our behaviour that new situations are a threat rather than an opportunity. Conversely, they may learn that new experiences are exciting and welcome rather than a cause for anxiety.

In the third scenario, the mother had her own history of finding separations difficult and her daughter's return to school was triggering this memory and also the accompanying emotions. In this case, it is the mother's own distress that is being expressed here, not the child's. The mother is having difficulty managing her own emotions and processing her own distress. First, she is setting a poor example for her daughter. Children learn by what they see. She is teaching her child that going back to school after the summer break is upsetting. She is teaching her child that this is the way to deal with distress: to seek comfort from a daughter. However, the chances are that she cannot help it. This mother needs to reflect on how she manages her pain and the impact that it has on her daughter if she is expressing this distress in her presence and taking solace from her embrace. She needs to learn to regulate her own emotions and do this in a space that is separate from her daughter. She needs to learn to anticipate those situations that will trigger this distress and plan accordingly. Perhaps she wasn't the best person to bring her daughter to school that day; perhaps it would have been better had she arranged for her daughter to be taken by someone else. Sometimes we have to realise our limitations and remove ourselves from a situation if we feel we can't manage it. And sometimes, we need help from others. We are all influenced by our histories. Difficult experiences leave their mark on us. Reminders of those experiences can easily trigger a tearful outburst. It is important for our own well-being and that of our children that we can identify these triggers and deal with the fallout. We may need to talk it through with a friend or partner; we may benefit from using a helpline; we may get guidance from self-help books; or we may need to get professional help through counselling or psychotherapy.

The final interpretation of the schoolyard scenario is that the mother was upset because the beginning of another school year was a marker that her daughter was getting older, becoming more and more her own person, and in some ways moving more and more away from the needy, dependent child that she enjoyed mothering so much. This is another example of how the parent's needs are superseding the child's. A parent who doesn't take delight in seeing their child become their own person has some serious self-reflection to do. The phrase whose life is it anyway? comes to mind. Most parents experience some nostalgia at seeing their child getting older – the cute, cuddly toddler is gone. As each new stage of development unfolds, there is a loss of what went before. It is important, however, that this is balanced by a welcoming of what is to come. Helping your child to become her own person is one of the most important challenges of parenting. Containing our emotional reaction to her getting older is therefore important, particularly when she is present. Children need to see us celebrate their growing independence. This will encourage them to embrace the future, providing they can do so in the knowledge that they have our blessing.

A final note about knowing yourself. As parents, we are strongly influenced by our experience of having being parented. If we have had a good overall experience of being parented, we may embrace this idea. We may be happy to acknowledge that we owe a lot to our parents for how we are as parents. We may have carried their value systems into our new families and strongly encourage our children to live by those same values. We may be aware that how we react to our children has a resonance with how our parents reacted to us. We may be able to acknowledge that, in some respects, our parents made mistakes. That they – like us – were a product of their time and that their beliefs on how to parent were influenced by what was then considered to be in the best interests of children. We may have different views on some issues, but overall we understand that we have been and continue to be affected by our parents.

On the other hand, we may have had a difficult experience of being parented. We may want to reject the idea that our own parenting is in any way influenced by our experiences as children. We may want to put as much distance as possible between how we are now and how we perceive our parents were then. Perhaps there were problems in our family of origin: alcohol or drug abuse, domestic violence, depression, anxiety or other mental health problems. Perhaps we have strived as parents to be different, to make sure that our children are not subjected to the kinds of experiences we had growing up. If this is the case, it is important to acknowledge that this in itself demonstrates how we have been influenced by our experiences of being parented and we can swing too far the other way. If our parents were extremely strict, we can veer too much in the other direction and be too lax, leaving our children feeling insecure and uncontained. If our parents were neglectful, we can be over-protective and smother our children, impeding their development and their natural instinctual drive towards independence. Peter Fonagy is a clinical psychologist in London who has carried out important studies with young parents from 'abusive' families. In his research with his colleagues he has highlighted a very important factor about how our past influences our present.[2] It is not the fact that we have had difficult experiences in the past that determines how we are as parents; rather, it is our ability to reflect on those experiences, our ability to acknowledge that we are affected in some ways by those experiences, and to make sense of those experiences, that influences the parents we are in the present.

---

2   P. Fonagy and M. Target (1997), 'Attachment and reflective function: Their role in self-organization', *Development and Psychopathology*. 4, pp. 679–700.

Remember ...

- Taking care of yourself will help you better take care of your children. You are your child's most powerful and influential role model. They will learn a lot more from what you do rather than from what you tell them to do.
- Check in with yourself to see how you're feeling from time to time. Listen to what your body is trying to tell you. Reflect on your thoughts, your feelings. This will help you to better recognise your child's thoughts and feelings. You will be able to trust your intuition about how your child is feeling. This will guide you to what they need.
- Take time each day to reflect on the little things you do well.
- Each day, prioritise some 'me time' so that you can spend some time doing something that gives you pleasure.
- Look for feedback from friends or others you trust.

TWO

Communication throughout Childhood and Adolescence

As children get older parents tend to focus more on the content of what they say. At an early age, we rely exclusively on their non-verbal communication. They communicate so much by their expressions, their tone of voice and their posture. We observe younger children closely in order to make sense of what's going on for them. We are sensitive to changes in their mood or their behaviour. We watch their play and know that this can be a window into their inner world, a theatre that enacts their thoughts, fantasies and worries. We can use these observations to get a sense of what is going on for our child. These cues are just as important as our children get older but sometimes the words get in the way. We can focus too much attention on what's being said, neglecting to watch out for the other forms of communication. At the same time our children are learning more and more to cover up their feelings and to talk their way through situations without showing too much of themselves. Sometimes parents have to be good detectives, thinking up various possibilities, testing these out, and being prepared to take risks and get it wrong.

Human beings are fascinating in that we are changing all the time. As our children grow from tiny tots to mature young adults, there are times of great transition and times of subtler shifts. In the early pre-school years, there is an obvious spurt in physical growth, language skills and cognitive development, with further bursts in the teenage years. In the middle childhood years, the pace of change slows down a little, as if there is time needed to process or consolidate the changes that have gone before and prepare the young person for those changes yet to come. There are pivotal times of transition: from home to playschool or school; from primary to secondary school; and from school to college or work. There are ever increasing social networks – friends, teachers, neighbours, coaches – who will have an influential impact on our child's development that extends beyond our domain. Helping our children navigate these transitions is an important task in parenting. How we ourselves have managed those changes in our own childhood and teenage years will impact on how we help our children to do it. Having support – friends or family to bounce ideas off and assist us in helping our children through these years – encourages us to do a better job. As children move from being quite dependent on us to developing their own sense of self, we talk with them in a different way. With some children we do more of the talking when they are younger and less of it as they get older. With others, we need to do much more listening and observing than talking. Psychoanalyst Ronald Fairbairn[3] has described human development as moving from immature dependency to mature dependency. I like this idea because it acknowledges that our children are always our children. They will always need us to be there for them, as someone to talk to or to be there to listen. Being mature and independent young adults does not mean that they don't still need us as their parents.

One of the best communication skills we can learn to develop is that of active listening; this involves listening with our whole bodies – maintaining eye contact, communicating through our facial expressions and demeanour – to highlight the fact that we are genuinely engaged in the conversation and interested in what the other party has to say. In active listening, we are using our eyes to see and our ears to hear. We are using our own feelings and reactions to what is being said to us to give us an idea of what the other person is feeling. Empathy, or trying to see things from another person's point of view, is an important component of active

---

3   Ronald Fairbairn, *Psychoanalytic Studies of the Personality*, (London: Psychology Press, 1952).

listening. Imagining what another person is feeling by listening to their communications enables us to be able to respond in a way that is helpful. Feeling listened to and feeling heard is a basic human need. This is why helplines are so popular. Having someone at the end of the phone who is able to communicate that they are really listening to you, gives you a sense that someone cares and that they are there for you in the midst of your distress.

Children are particularly sensitive to the way in which adults listen to them. When they are trying to communicate with us and we appear distracted, we can give off the wrong message: that we are not interested in what they have to say. It may be that we are simply tied up with another activity or have something else on our minds. For instance, a frown that simply indicates we are trying to process something could be interpreted by a child as a sign of disapproval. As children get older they develop the ability to read cues (such as facial expressions) and to read them correctly. Children who are very sensitive or insecure or who have had certain difficult life experiences will be more likely to read these cues in a negative way. In this sense, they may 'expect the worst'. For such children it is important to watch out for signs that they may be misinterpreting us, or 'reading our minds' but getting it wrong. We need to really listen to them. We can then help them say these thoughts out loud so that we can correct them and reassure them. If they interpret our response as one of disinterest or disapproval they may be reluctant to try again. So sometimes we have to be able to anticipate what message they might be getting from us, and respond accordingly. For instance, if we are busy preparing dinner when they are trying to show us work they did in school that day, it is advisable to say so: sorry, I just want to get this done now. Can we look at that after we've had dinner? If you have a tendency to forget, ask them to remind you: can you remind me to look at that after dinner? That looks really good but I can't look at it right now.

In this chapter, I highlight some of the key features of different stages of development from the preschool years through to adolescence. This is not intended to be an in-depth account of child and adolescent development. Rather, I discuss some of the salient features of these stages in light of how we communicate with our children. It's important that we grow with our children, that we respect their various needs, while also acknowledging how the demands of parenthood change as our children grow.

The Preschool Years

Communication with our children begins in the womb. Stress during pregnancy has a significant impact on both mother and child. We know that the intra-uterine world is acutely sensitive to the mother's emotional well-being and that the baby in the womb is responsive to sound, light and vibration, be it soothing or otherwise. It is in the way we hold them while feeding, the eye contact, and the gentle calming voice that we help them develop a sense of themselves as individuals who are loved and cared for. During the early years, our children's communication skills are developing rapidly. Long before children say their first words they are communicating with us through eye contact, expressions of pleasure or distress and by communicating their needs or responding to us in their own unique manner. Babies cry to let us know that something is wrong – they are in pain, they are wet, they are hungry, they are tired. Parents sometimes come to recognise the different kinds of crying that signal what is wrong. I'm wet; I'm sore; I'm hungry; I'm tired. Through the process of what we call 'attunement', parents and carers get to know their children and their own idiosyncratic means of communicating. From an early age, children need their parents or carers to put words on these feelings for them. Oh dear, you're tired, time for a sleep, a parent may say to their six-month-old baby. The child may not at this age understand the meaning of the words, but they understand the message through the tone of voice and the attendant behaviour of the parent.

Babies will show their interest in the world by looking around and maintaining eye contact with those parts of their environment that interest them, while looking away when they are not interested or when something upsets them. There is a YouTube video clip demonstrating Ed Tronick's 'still face experiment'[4] with a mother and her one-year-old baby showing how this attunement works, but more importantly, showing how actively engaged the baby is in these interactions. A mother and baby are engaged in reciprocal communication through playful facial expressions of delight. The mother then suddenly stops reacting to her baby by maintaining a neutral facial expression. The baby responds within seconds, trying everything in her repertoire to get the mother's attention but to no avail – the mother's expression remains neutral. The baby then gets distressed, crying out and flailing her arms. When the mother resumes her play, the baby reverts to playful interaction immediately. This is an example of how non-verbal communication can be so powerful, how important it is for infants to be responded to in their interpersonal interactions, and the active role that children from a young age have in directing these interactions. It helps us understand that children are engaged with us as their parents – they are both affected by us and they have an impact on us.

Interacting with babies and small children is important for their language development but also their social and emotional development. A parent who goes about their daily chores, chatting all the while to their infant child, is helping that child's communication capacities. The baby is getting the message that they are an essential part of their parent's life. The baby is also being 'held in mind', a process that we know is important for an individual's psychological development.

4   https://www.youtube.com/watch?v=apzXGEbZhto

In these early days before the child can communicate verbally, parents draw heavily on their intuition and instinctively name emotions for their child: oh you're hungry, you poor thing. Mummy forgot the time. Naming children's feelings for them in the early years gives them the language to be able to name their own feelings later on. Repeated experiences such as this contribute to the development of the baby's personality. They learn through these experiences to be self-sufficient. It is not just the words used but the tone of voice and the intuitive intervention of the parents. All together, these convey to the child an understanding of their emotional state. For the baby, being understood by her parent helps the developing child make sense of her own feelings and come to understand herself. Feeling heard and understood is important for her emotional development.

Even when children develop verbal skills, they still communicate a lot through their behaviour. Watching our children play either by themselves or with other children can give us many clues as to how they are navigating various situations in their daily lives. Children often use toys and play materials to work through their feelings, to re-enact the scenarios that they are living through and to test different solutions to the challenges they are playing out with these materials. Children will use dolls to represent parents and children and how they interact with each other. They will use toy animals to illustrate adventures. Their play is meaningful and will often reflect how they are thinking and feeling. Watching children play gives parents a window into their inner worlds. Often children are not able to recognise their feelings so it is not just about whether they have the labels to name them. It is often left to parents to guess how their child is feeling and to look for feedback from their child as to whether they got it right.

As the baby develops and begins to use their first words, the reaction of parents to the child's attempts at speech will influence the pattern of communication that follows. Encouraging children to talk about their thoughts and feelings from the beginning helps to establish this routine for later years. We can do this by setting example – talking about our own thoughts and feelings; and by encouraging them when they are talking to us. Responding to children's questions as best we can when they are younger will encourage them to continue asking those questions as they grow and mature.

The Primary School Years

A whole new world opens up to the child when they go to school. This is both exciting and frightening for many children. As one of the key transitions a child will experience in their early years, it's important that they manage it well. As a big developmental step, it provides an opportunity for a child to experience success. Therefore it is worth investing some time and effort into creating the best possible opportunities for them to ensure that it does go well. Talking with children about starting school helps to create a space for them to express whatever worries they might have about this big step in their lives. Sometimes parents worry about putting ideas into their child's head – that if the child hasn't said anything about it, maybe it's best to leave well enough alone. As a general rule this is not such a good idea. It is better to put things out there, to name possible anxieties and worries. If this does apply to your child, they are more likely to use this as an opportunity to express their own worries.

Sometimes it's a good idea to introduce the idea of children being afraid to go to school by referring to another child (real or fictional) who may have these worries. I was talking to someone at work today. Her little girl is starting school too. She's a bit upset about it. She's scared of being in such a big class ... do you ever think about that? or My friend's little boy is finding it hard to go to sleep at night. He's thinking about school a lot. He's worried whether he is going to make friends.

By talking about another child, you can create a little bit of distance in order to help your own child feel safer talking about their worries. Talking about other children's feelings is not as overwhelming as talking about their own feelings.

It's also essential to ensure we create a good relationship with our child's teachers; they spend so much time with our children, they can notice things that we don't see ourselves. They have the added benefit of observing how our child copes and interacts when faced with dealing with their peers, often in large numbers. Parent–teacher meetings are a great opportunity to get feedback on how another significant adult in our child's life experiences them. It is also an opportunity to share with teachers how we experience our children. This way, together, as parents and teachers we can all help create opportunities for communication with our children.

As children learn more and more about the world they live in through their classes in school, they ask more and more questions at home. Parents can use these 'question time' sessions to explore with children how they think about these issues. As well as reinforcing the atmosphere in the home that encourages open discussion, it also creates an opportunity to explore how children feel about new ideas and challenges. This can then extend into more sensitive topics that will also be raised in the school curriculum – relationships with peers, bullying or child abuse. If children are accustomed to discussing how they feel about events that are happening in the world, it will be easier for them to talk about sensitive issues much closer to home.

Even for the child who has attended play school, there is a marked move 'up a gear' in terms of the challenges that the transition to primary education presents: having to sit in class and pay attention; co-operating with other children; conforming to socially-acceptable behaviour; managing the play environment of the schoolyard. These early school years also typically represent a gradual move away from the early dependency on parents – the child may have younger siblings so there is less attention to go around; he will hopefully make new friends in school resulting in his playing in other children's houses. How a young child adapts to this major transition will to some extent influence how they negotiate other transitions in life. One child may have the capacity to welcome new experiences openly while another may approach with caution, triggering the fears of loss experienced at an earlier age.

Along with the potential pleasures this new world brings, it also brings challenges that the child may struggle to overcome. At this age children are beginning to be more aware of their feelings as their own, as distinct from their parents'. They are now able to make connections between how they feel and what they are thinking. During these years, the child is learning to manage their own intense feelings and also manage their social world – to behave in a socially acceptable way. The structure and rules of games, so typical of this age, can be seen as indicative of this struggle. By developing new skills, the child experiences a newfound sense of competence and control over their lives. The repetitive and monotonous activities so characteristic of these years serve a function: they help the child put order on his world. To deny this and simply try to get your child to behave differently is to deny his feelings, to tell him his feelings don't matter. As the child is often unaware himself of why he feels the need to obsess about a particular game or repeat certain routines, the onus is on the parent to intuit what may be going on.

Why might they need to play the same game over and over? Why do they get so upset when someone doesn't play by the rules? What might be troubling them?

Sometimes these rigid routines are about seeking safety. Routine brings predictability and constancy and while children generally need this a little more at this age, it may be that your own child needs it even more at this point in time. Keeping things in order can bring a feeling of safety, a sense of security and control. It can be a way of protecting ourselves from strong or intense emotions that we fear will overwhelm us. We all need to learn how to manage intense feelings.

Adolescence

The World Health Organisation defines adolescence as the period of childhood encompassing the ages of ten to nineteen. The teenage years are often a period marked by a profound sense of tension as the individual looks both outwards and inwards: outwards in the sense that their social network is attracting them away from home towards friends with whom they readily confide; inwards insofar as they may be more self-conscious than they were in their earlier years. They are sometimes acutely aware of all the physical changes going on in their bodies. For many this can be confusing and hard to articulate. Because of their advanced cognitive ability, they are learning more and more to problem-solve, to be able to see things from other people's perspectives, to engage in conversations about alternative possibilities. This represents a broadening of their horizons that often prompts lots of questions. The moodiness associated with teenage years starts now. Some young people can appear more withdrawn, retreating to their room or listening to music that cuts out communication with parents. Parents can feel excluded from their teenagers' lives and this can be hurtful. Parents may be grieving the loss of the child who came to them for everything, and welcomed a hug or a cuddle.

Speaking with our children from an early age and putting words on their feelings is important for their language development but it is also crucial for their ability to recognise their own feelings and their ability to develop a sense of themselves and how they feel. It is through this process that the child is able to internalise this skill over time and later come to learn how to name their own feelings for themselves. This ability develops differently in different people. Most children get better at it as they get older.

But during the teenage years, as young people struggle with the various ways in which they are developing so rapidly, they can come to need extra help in this area. They may need their parents to read them and be able to notice what's going on and put words on it for them. The younger child may not benefit from your wild guesses as to how they are feeling but as long as you get it mostly right, you won't be doing any harm. The teenager, however, if misunderstood, may feel very hurt and maligned. The mis-attunement at this stage of life can be the perfect trigger for a heated row. You never understand me! You never listen! You know nothing! Many adults continue to struggle with being able to put words on their feelings, particularly if they have experienced a trauma along the way. We know from research in neuroscience that when a person experiences an emotional trauma, the parts of their brain that are associated with this skill of being able to name feelings can be affected.

Often teenagers feel as though they are on an emotional rollercoaster. Many appear angry and irritable. This can be their way of struggling with feelings that are confusing. Teenagers may turn towards their friends for support, telling them about their thoughts and feelings instead of confiding in their parents. They may feel that their friends will understand them better. Shared experiences can help young people confide in their friends before they consider confiding in an adult. They know that if they tell an adult something that may have consequences, there is a higher risk that 'something will be done about it'. They may not be sure they want an adult to intervene and so may feel safer in talking to friends than parents. At a time when they desire more autonomy in their lives, withholding information from parents is one way of exercising control. For parents, this can feel like rejection. They may have a sense that something is going on for the young person but may not be able to get them to talk about it. Parents can feel redundant or superfluous. What is really important at times like these is for parents to understand that they have to hang in there. Their children do need their support but sometimes have a funny way of showing it. What is really important is that parents don't withdraw in reaction to their teenage child's withdrawal. They should remain close enough so that the young person doesn't have to work too hard to reach them; distant enough that the young person doesn't feel pressurised to engage.

Challenging parents' views and pushing against their limits is a typical pattern at this age. They are better able to argue. They are now able to conceive of different possibilities and generate different solutions to problems. In many ways, they challenge parental notions of right and wrong to see how well they stand up to critique. Questioning parents' authority is part of an ongoing struggle to find their place in the world. Pushing the boundaries can help young people get a sense of where their space begins and ends. Beginning to see how parents don't keep their own rules is also characteristic of this period of development. Spending time with their own gender is part of consolidating their identity – what it means to be a girl or boy. They can be very idealistic, very black and white in their thinking, showing a tendency to generalise that appears unfair. It's almost as if the discovery of how few real certainties there are in life leads them to cling on to whatever ones they can. Often they get this wrong – but arguing with them is simply getting drawn into the wrong conversation. Parents need to see beyond the words spoken to the feelings that are being expressed. Generalisations such as you're always saying that or you never listen to my side need to be understood as I'm frustrated or I don't feel heard here or even I don't seem to be able to control what's happening and that really frustrates me. They can be very authoritative, and 'the expert on everything' as they experiment with all their new-found knowledge. This can really press our buttons. Who do they think they are, suddenly knowing it all? The transition from the role of the parent who is looked up to as a font of wisdom to one whose opinion barely matters can result in an argument or a 'power struggle' that spirals into a full-blown row. The tension between not wanting to tolerate unacceptable behaviour (and perhaps responding by resorting to punishment) and understanding that the young person is really struggling (and responding with support) is difficult to manage for parents.

At this stage, young people are discovering those 'truths' that they once accepted unopposed are actually open to challenge, that their parents can be, and often are, wrong. Rules that were taken for granted in families are now up for debate. Young people may demand explanations for these rules. Adolescence is a time when young people become keenly aware of justice and injustice. Rules have to be fair. While these same rules may have been accepted without question in the past, they are now open to scrutiny. What may be fair for a young child may not be fair for a teenager. They may not have the intellectual capacities to see these arguments through and their passion may turn to frustration and irritability or anger. On occasion, their ability to articulate may surpass their ability to reflect and the words come out of their mouths without thought.

For parents, it's important to engage with their teenage children in these debates. They are looking for a challenge and they need someone to present that challenge for them. It is so much safer for them to play this out at home, in their own family. You might even consider it a compliment if your child is rude, obnoxious and misbehaved at home. The expression 'we take it out on the ones we love' is very true of children and teenagers. They do tend to act out their anxieties and aggression at home, where it is safe to do so. In a way, there is permission to do this, albeit not explicitly so – we don't tell our toddlers: I don't mind if you have a temper tantrum in the middle of the supermarket aisle with everybody watching me lose my patience or our teenagers: sure, it's fine to shout and roar at me or I'm quite happy for you to bang the door so hard it almost comes off its hinges. But we do –

hopefully – tell them that no matter how they are with us, we will still love them. They don't risk jeopardising their relationship with us if they're having a bad day and behave as if they are really not a very nice person. In many respects, 'if you can get through it they can'. At this age, the risk of humiliation is high – if they get it wrong or if they can't 'win', they need to be able to save face. It's important to understand that this is a normal part of development. It does not reflect a personality trait. When their teenage son appears arrogant, the parent needs to see this in the context of this development. Their behaviour may well be arrogant but this does not mean their child has turned into a stranger. In developing their personality, they are testing out different ways of being, trying to find themselves. The swings that parents see in their child's temperament represents this struggle that teenagers engage in while developing their identity.

It's important for parents to listen and be supportive and understand that this is just the way it is for the moment. Expecting young people at this age to be consistent in their attitudes and behaviour is unrealistic and unfair. Typically, teenagers have a lot of questions to ask of their parents. Whether they will ask them or not will depend to a large extent on what atmosphere has been created from their early years in the home. Is this a family where children's questions are welcomed? Will they be listened to and heard? Will they be judged? Will the parent be able to contain the conversation without getting really upset or worried? Giving them more responsibility within the family helps to stretch them in a way that meets this need of pushing limits. It also gives them a message that they are to be trusted, that they can be relied on, which increases their sense of competence and promotes their self-esteem.

Remember ...

✳ Establish family routines that foster communication. Conversations at mealtimes help reinforce the message that parents are interested in their children's lives and in what they have to say.

✳ Seize every opportunity to encourage conversation. Find opportunities to do things with them that they enjoy. Sometimes, not having to make eye contact is good as it makes the experience less intense – walking along the street together or chatting while you are driving the car is a good way of achieving this.

✳ Don't take it personally if your older child dismisses what you say. This may be part of their way of managing it for themselves. If you notice that you constantly seem to be 'giving out' to your child, try to find an opportunity to praise them for something they have done well. Get them to explain things to you that they are learning about. For some children you will need to voice their thoughts and feelings, to put words on their emotions for them, while other children need some space to do this for themselves. Children rely heavily on their parents for information. Forewarned is forearmed. Young people need accurate information. If they are left to rely on their friends to learn about life, the information may be confusing at best and inaccurate at worst.

✳ Grow with your child: welcome each new stage of development with open arms and the excitement and awe that it deserves. You need to both lead and follow.

THREE

Talking with Children about Separation

Many parents struggle with how best to help their children navigate the territory of separation. Most parents find this process painful and difficult themselves. Often though, their main worry is for their children: will it do harm? How can I make it as painless as possible? Will there be permanent damage to my child? An important point to remember is that we cannot completely protect our children from painful experiences. Life can be difficult. Children need to learn how to deal with such pain. There is no avoiding it. And if parents try to deny their children this experience, they are actually denying them the opportunity to learn how to deal with their pain. Our early lessons in dealing with emotional pain stay with us and each difficult experience we have to deal with is to some extent dependent on what went before – how we dealt with it last time around. As we get older, we develop the skills to deal with such pain in our own individual way. Our parents, however, were our first role models. So we learned (or didn't learn) early in life, based on how they themselves coped and how they taught us to cope.

One of the best and most obvious ways of ensuring that your child is not too adversely affected by your separation is if parents work together. Given that many couples are in conflict at this particular time, it can be very challenging to put differences aside and plan how to deal with the separation in such a way that it minimises the hurt to the children. We know from research[5] with

---

5   S. M. Greene, E. R. Anderson, M. S. Forgatch, D. S. DeGarmo and E. M. Hetherington: 'Risk and Resilience after Divorce', *Normal Family Processes, Growing Diversity and Complexity* (New York: The Guilford Pressm, 2003), pp. 96–120.

children that those who have adapted well to the transition during separation and divorce have supportive, communicative parents. Parents who explain to their children what is going to happen can help them to adjust to the changes ahead. Parents need to sit down with their children, explain that they are separating and make it very clear that the children are in no way responsible, that they as a couple no longer love each other in the same way but that they DO love their children. Parents need to give their children a very clear message that they as adults are responsible for the separation and that they as adults will take responsibility for any changes that this will bring about in their child's life.

If parents are able to manage their own distress over the breakdown of their relationship, it can go a long way to ensuring that the process is as tolerable as possible for their children. Children will respond in different ways, so it is important not to pre-judge how they will react to this major life event or presume to know how to help them best. Talking with them about the process; giving them information about what's happening, whenever possible; encouraging them to talk about their feelings and thoughts about the process; and providing reassurance to them over time will help them both in the short term and in the longer term.

Know Yourself
Many adults struggle with co-parenting, even when their own relationship is going well. When a couple is entrenched in a separation, it is particularly challenging. In addition to dealing with the change in their own relationship, they have to establish a new relationship: that of parenting their children while not being together. Many things that have been taken for granted are no longer so. Conversations are needed to develop a plan to ensure that parents can give their children the best possible opportunity not to suffer unduly from the breakup of the relationship. Often when parents separate there is conflict and they don't necessarily want to talk to each other; this can

prevent them from noticing the hurt experienced by their children. One or other parent is often in incredible pain. This pain drives them to lash out at the other parent in a bid to punish them for bringing the situation about. Sometimes one parent may feel very strongly that if the other parent has, for instance, had an affair he or she shouldn't be allowed to spend time with the children. They have done wrong. They are the cause of all this hurt. They have hurt the children as well as their partner. They shouldn't be allowed to continue life 'as normal'. They should be punished. Generally, attempts to punish the 'offending' partner also means the child is punished too.

Despite the challenges, talking to each other is essential if parents want to put the children's needs first. It is the breakdown in communication that often leaves children hurt – lack of information, misinterpretations, broken promises. Clear communication between parents is essential. Parents often send messages to each other through their children. This is generally not a good idea. Direct communication is best, preferably through face-to-face conversation. Text messages by their nature are brief and leave a lot of room for interpretation and misunderstanding. Important information may need to be communicated by email or letter but it is important to reflect on the tone of such communications as the written word can be much colder and starker than the spoken word, and may provoke a reaction that exacerbates the situation.

Sometimes when couples separate, one parent (usually the father) may then spend more time with the children than before. They may begin to notice things for the first time – little habits or routines that the mother has been practising all along but have now come into focus for the father. He may find that he doesn't agree with this approach, now that he is paying attention to it, and now that he is expected to behave in the same way, for the sake of consistency. If children are accustomed to certain routines, such as those around mealtimes and bedtimes, it is really important that they are kept consistent during the transition period, even if a parent does not agree that this is the best practice. Think of it in terms of how we cope with new things or new people. Sometimes when we are under a lot of stress, keeping things the same helps us to cope. Having to manage new people and new situations often feels too demanding on the limited resources we have at that time. It takes too much effort. Now that each parent is taking individual responsibility for implementing parenting practices they will find themselves wanting to do it in the way that they believe is best for their children or in the way that suits their lifestyle better. If changes are to be made, it is usually better to give the children some time to adjust before introducing new routines. As children adapt to the newly-constructed family unit, they will be better able to cope with differing routines when they are more settled in themselves and have successfully coped with the transition of the separation process. Maintaining consistency throughout this time can help them feel more secure. Sometimes the consistency is more important than 'doing the right thing'.

All separations bring some sort of loss. No matter how 'positive' the change may be seen by parents, it still constitutes the loss of whatever went before. Even when there is violence, substance abuse or addictions, a separation can be experienced with great pain. There is not only the loss of the family unit as they knew it, but the loss of a shared future as a family. Separation can mean the end of that dream. People sometimes feel a sense of failure when things don't work out – a 'failed marriage' is not what they imagined when they first made those wedding vows. The changes that follow a separation can be seismic – change of home, change of community, change of friends. Parents have their own adjustments to make which are often difficult. They may have ambivalent feelings about the decision to separate, wondering if this is going to be for the best in the longer term, trying to reassure themselves that they have made the right choice. For many, it isn't their decision to make – it has been foisted upon them. Adjusting to this reality can be difficult and most people need a lot of support to carry them through it. Being there for others when you are going through such a tough time yourself is not easy. At a time when you are experiencing a lot of turmoil and stress, it can feel overwhelming to have to be more present for your children. Older children may appear anxious and worried about the future and very much focused on the potential setbacks. At the very time that they need most for you to be calm, in charge, and confident about the future, you may be feeling panicked, out of control and anxious. It may be a good idea to consider whether you need additional support yourself to help you through this time. Support from friends and family may not be enough for you, particularly if you are reluctant to discuss the difficulties you are having with those who know you and your ex-partner. You could think about using helplines or online discussion groups on parenting websites (such as www.rollercoaster.ie). You could look for a support group that may be available in your area. Individual counselling might help you to manage your own feelings and support you as you try to support your children.

Children can suffer in the longer term from parental separation and this does to some extent depend on how the parents have managed the situation. Sometimes parents are so hurt and so angry with each other that they cannot bring themselves to put their children first. They are not able to see the harm they are doing to their children by expressing their anger at the other parent. They often, unwittingly, take this out on their children or use them as scapegoats in the tug-of-war with their ex-partner. Often, parents don't realise they are doing this: they may need a good friend to point this out to them. They may genuinely believe that they are doing what's best for their children. They simply cannot see that their bitterness and anger are clouding their judgement. Well-meaning friends who try to help them see this can be cast out and perceived as taking the other parent's side or as lacking in understanding – just at the time they are most needed.

Being aware of your own feelings is very challenging when going through a separation. Avoiding such feelings can seem like a more palatable choice – I'll just get on with the business of coping and worry about how I feel later. However, how we feel influences how we are as parents. If we are not paying attention to our own feelings, there is a danger that they will get in the way when we are trying to help our children pay attention to theirs. Having friends and family to bounce ideas off or simply to offload onto can help us separate out our own feelings from what our children may be feeling. If our children see that we are looking after ourselves, they will be less likely to concern themselves with how we are feeling. Being calm and being able to set our own feelings aside while we sit and talk with children will give them the space they need to express their own feelings and thoughts without having to worry too much about us.

Know Your Child
Children need most of all to be loved, to be cared for, and to believe that their world is safe and predictable. Providing security and stability can be challenging during times of change. When life is not so stable, it can be difficult to ensure that children feel safe and secure. So it is important for parents to think firstly about each particular child and what they need to feel safe and secure, and then what aspects of the child's life can be kept stable and consistent. Each child is different and will respond to change in different ways. Their own unique personalities will, to some extent, dictate how they deal with and react to change. It is not possible to predict these reactions – the best thing to do is to know your own child, how they typically react to changes, and try to use your knowledge about them to uncover how best to help them through this change.

Routines are great for helping children feel secure in themselves. They bring predictability to daily life that takes on great importance during times of turbulence. Some children will need this stability more than others, particularly children who are prone to anxiety. They may need this more than other children who are able to take change in their stride. Simple routines need to be kept up such as maintaining consistency in meals (this is not the time to try out new lunches or dinners), collecting children from school, letting children have friends over or letting them go to friends' houses and do extra-curricular activities. Sometimes the separation can result in some of these activities becoming more impractical to maintain. A balance needs to be struck between the potential benefits of maintaining a routine and making life easier for the adults concerned. Sometimes it is necessary to put up with considerable inconvenience in order to keep children's routines going for as long as possible.

Very young children may show fearful reactions and extra clinginess. Older children may also show sadness, embarrassment, relief, anger and guilt. For children in the 'middle childhood' years, fairness is important – most children will not want to be seen to favour either parent and so will be concerned that arrangements are seen to be fair. They can also be preoccupied with who is to blame for the break-up. Their questions may probe this and so it is important that parents are prepared and agree a strategy on how to respond. Repeating the same response over and over will usually succeed in putting an end to these questions, for example, Mum and Dad have agreed that we can't live together any more. It just didn't work out. Children at this age will also tend to feel insecure and be easily upset if their routine is not maintained. It is not unusual for children to encounter peer difficulties, tummy aches, headaches or bed-wetting as they struggle through this process. They don't tend to share as much with their peers as the older group of teenagers and may not be as likely to turn to their parents as they did when they were younger. Children in these middle childhood years may also feel embarrassed if they don't have other friends who have gone through a separation. They may feel ashamed that their parents are splitting up.

Older children may want to know if there is someone else involved. Parents need to agree what is best to say if this is the case. It may be that one parent is involved with another partner and that the children will be meeting that person in the near future. Honesty is very important in these instances. Being caught out in a lie will not provide a good foundation for the new relationships that have to be developed between parents and children following separation.

It is also important not to expect a particular reaction. Children need space and time to take in all this information. They are entitled to have their own unique reactions. They may or may not get upset. It's really important that you don't read too much into their reaction at this stage. Children will need space over time and opportunities to talk about it with each parent as and when they are ready. Some of these questions may be possible to answer and some of them may not. It is best to be honest and it is important to give them whatever information you can. You may not know what is going to happen but you do know that you will continue to love them and to look out for them. You can say that you will try your hardest not to bring too many changes into their lives. You may not be able to discuss why it is that you are separating. This is a private matter between you and your partner and giving children a clear message that you are not going to discuss this is better than just avoiding the conversation. If you don't know, then say so. Or if you haven't decided yet, then say so. Children are often grasping for certainty in asking these questions. If you give them certainty where there is none, you risk hurting them if the decision doesn't turn out as you expected. If you don't give them any information, you risk leaving it to their imagination and that can be a lot more frightening than the reality.

Listen
Parents need to pay particular attention to their children during this transition. Sometimes parents think that pre-verbal children are too young to know what is going on and therefore cannot be

distressed by what's happening. Babies are very sensitive to what is happening in their carers' worlds. If a parent is distressed, the infant can pick this up and sense the distress around him or her. The process is likely to be difficult for the parent so children of all ages will be acutely sensitive to their parents' feelings. The older child may be reluctant to openly talk about or express their distress for fear of upsetting their parents. They may feel that to be sad about what is happening is not okay, that it may in some way represent a betrayal. They may feel angry towards their parents, not understanding why their parents can't just 'make up'. It can be very difficult for some children to express that anger as they may fear the consequences. Such children may show this anger or other less palatable feelings through their play with toys or in their peer relationships. Watching out for such expressions of emotion is important. Encouraging younger children to engage with their play materials or to draw pictures about how they feel can be helpful. They can provide a gateway into conversations about these difficult feelings that your child may be having.

Watching your child closely during this transition will give you clues as to how they are feeling. There may be changes in sleeping and eating patterns, school work may be affected, friendships may suffer. The quiet introverted child may become more withdrawn or the outgoing boisterous child may become even more gregarious. Or the quiet well-behaved child may suddenly start acting out, getting into fights or rows with friends, while the typically more sociable child becomes quiet and withdrawn. Reflecting on your child's behaviour, watching out for signs of distress, and thinking about how this behaviour may reflect their feelings about the situation will help you to initiate conversations with them about how they are coping and what you can do to help them cope better.

Giving children attention and permission to express themselves shows them that we care, that we are interested in what they have to say and that it is okay to have these feelings, whatever they are.

If children are struggling to put words on their feelings, make some suggestions (being careful at all times that you are sensing what they are feeling, rather than voicing what you are feeling yourself) and check out if you are right. You might say: you look a bit sad today. Are you okay? or I noticed you didn't go out playing with your friends. Do you prefer to just be by yourself? or you seem a big angry. Would you like to talk about it? or even you seem a bit angry with me. I guess things have changed a lot around here. That must be hard for you.

In the midst of a conflictual separation process, it can be easy for one parent to think that their child really doesn't need to spend much time with the other parent. Perhaps the parent who is no longer living in the family home didn't spend much time with the child when they did live there. However, the meaning of a relationship bears only a tenuous connection with the quantity of time spent together – this is why we talk of quality time not quantity time. Children may want to spend more time with the parent who left – to help them feel secure in this relationship. Or they may feel angry with the parent who left and refuse to see them. Children may be angry with either parent and feel protective of another, or they may feel angry with both parents. It is difficult to really listen to children who are experiencing feelings that are so different from our own. If these feelings don't make sense to us, it can be easy to misinterpret them, to not really hear them and therefore not respond to what they need. If we think of it symbolically, it is like placing our feelings on a shelf, taking them and setting them aside, leaving us 'clear' or open to hearing or sensing how our children are feeling. Knowing that children can have different reactions may help, so reading up about how children typically respond to separation can be useful for parents, always bearing in mind that each child is different and your child may not be reacting in a typical way.

Listening to your child does not mean allowing them to dictate. It is important to stick to arrangements as planned and not be swayed by children who may express their feelings through rebelling, for example by objecting to spending time with a parent. This can be the child's way of trying to take control of a situation within which they feel powerless. However, while the child may feel more powerful in the short term, if parents concede to their wishes to change arrangements, the message the child is really getting is that their parents are not able to control the situation, that they in fact are in charge, and that can leave them feeling very overwhelmed and unsafe. Parents need to work together on this and present a united front. They need to expect that their child may throw a tantrum; they need to meet this with patience and warm authority and they need to stand firm and show their child that they are in charge and that everything will be okay.

However, the response needed here does vary with age. As with parenting in general, younger children depend more on their parents to know what is best for them. Older children and teenagers, while still needing their parents to make many decisions on their behalf, also need to be heard and their views taken into account when making such decisions. Sometimes when young people are very angry with a parent, they need some space to come to terms with what is happening. Being forced into contact with a parent can be unhelpful. This is a delicate situation to manage and there are no absolute rights and wrongs. Sometimes, listening to children means letting their wishes take precedence.

Ask

Parents worry about what is too much to say and what is too little. No one can really decide this except for parents themselves. They know their children best and they need to tailor the conversation to each child, taking account of their child's age, their child's temperament and personality and how they think their child may react. While it is important to stick to the facts, this might be too much for one child to absorb in one conversation. In this case, it may be necessary to have a few brief discussions about the separation over a period of a few days. If children get very distressed, it's probably best to halt the conversation and give them time to recover a little before sharing more information with them.

It is always a good idea to reflect on the question: how much does my child need to know right now? This question is often answered by children themselves if they are given the space and the permission to ask their own questions. A parent needs to know what worries their child has about the separation. Giving children time and space to get their heads around something as big as this is important. Telling children sooner rather than later is good. It's best to get there before your children start wondering too much. As I mentioned earlier, children's imaginations can be vivid and it's worth pre-empting their anxiety by keeping them in the loop as much as possible.

That said, refrain from making definitive statements until you are certain what course of action is to be taken. Children need clarity from you, rather than vague speculations. When you have made a decision, it's best to tell your children as soon as you can. Having a clear plan of action and a time frame in the event of, say, moving home will help your child process any major changes. This needs to be a planned conversation. It is important to give some thought to how you will do this. How do you normally speak with your children? Who usually does the talking? It's usually best to follow your usual routine, but it is important that both parents contribute. If one partner stays silent, this can give the child the idea that the decision was one-sided and it may sow seeds of doubt or inspire the hope that perhaps the separation won't happen after all. It is important that you have agreed and that you don't contradict each other, even if you feel the urge to. The important message you want to convey is: Mum and Dad are no longer happy together and have decided to separate. This is a decision you have made together, between the two of you, and has nothing to do with the children. The children are not in any way to blame for what has happened. You will continue to love them just as much as before. Separating will not change this. You will always be there for them, no matter what.

Conversations about 'big issues' that involve both parents are better for children. When adults speak individually to children, they tend to put their own 'spin' on what they say. They are speaking from their own individual perspective. It is difficult to get a unified message across if each parent is communicating separately with their child.

Children tend to have different fears at different ages. Children of all ages can blame themselves so the clear message that it is not their fault always needs to be given and reinforced many times. However, younger children are more prone to this as they still think in ways that we call 'egocentric', that is, that they are the centre of the world and therefore everything that happens in the world is to do with them. While this is all part and parcel of a child's emotional development, it may mean they feel too much responsibility for what goes on in their lives. Younger children therefore need repeated reassurance that they are in no way to blame for events. Older children are better able to conceive of the possibility that their parents simply don't love each other in the same way anymore.

If one parent is going to live elsewhere, younger children may fear that they are not going to see this parent again. In this case, an agreement about how much time the non-resident parent will spend with the children is important to sort out in advance. Children will need reassurance as to when they will see the parent. If this parent can be involved in the children's daily activities it is all the better. This will provide the continuity that is needed. As many things as possible need to stay the same: the child will have enough change to cope with.

Reassure

Lots and lots of reassurance is needed. Everything is going to be okay – this is the message you want to convey to your children. You are not to blame. You can talk to me about this any time you want. And if you don't want to talk, that's okay too.

When children react with anger or distress, it is important to acknowledge these feelings and not jump in to try to make them feel better. Reassuring children too quickly is giving them the message that it's not okay to feel upset or angry. They need their feelings validated – it's okay to feel this way and it's okay to say so. If your child doesn't show any reaction, sometimes it's a good idea to name some possible feelings – that they might feel sad or upset or angry and if they want to talk about this at another time, that's fine.

While it is important to listen carefully to children at this difficult time, it is important not to give them the impression that they have a say in what's going to happen if this is not the case. At times of stress children cling to what their parents say. This is partly why it is so difficult when promises are broken. Sometimes parents don't even realise what they have said and are taken aback at the intense reaction they get from their child when plans are changed. What is important to understand is that many of us become quite rigid in our thinking when we feel anxious. The more anxious we feel, the more rigidly we cling to our expectations and the more thrown we feel when things don't go according to plan. When a child reacts dramatically to a change in plan, it is not just this change they are reacting to. Sometimes it can feel like a rug being pulled from under them. Their world is being turned upside down. Any other change – no matter how small it may seem to others – may feel like the last straw for them. This is particularly so if there are arrangements in place for parents to visit their children or to do things together. It may be that due to work commitments a parent has to change their plans to do something with their child. Unfortunately, children can interpret this as meaning that their parent doesn't love them anymore. The message that is given is not necessarily the message that is received. A change in time or decision to go somewhere different may seem like a minor adjustment for a parent, but for the child it may evoke feelings of uncertainty and insecurity, resulting in angry outbursts or floods of tears. Parents need to see this reaction in the context of what is going on for the family and how difficult it is to manage the transition. Sticking rigidly to plans may be a good idea to help children through the most difficult time of the process.

It is important for children to feel some sense of agency in their lives – that what they think or say makes a difference. However, it is also important that the burden of making decisions is not placed on their shoulders. In some families, there is the option of living with either parent. For younger children it is important that this decision is made by the parents and that they are not asked to choose where they will live. The decision needs to be based on what is in the child's best interests. Older children and teenagers will have a view on this issue, and while their views need to be taken into consideration, again it is important that they understand that the decision on this rests with their parents. A decision of where to live must not be seen as choosing one parent over another.

At times like these, children benefit from support from outside the family. There may be a Rainbows programme[6] available in their school or some other outlet that will support them through this difficult time. Being in a group with other children will help them express their own feelings and thoughts, and by hearing about other children's experiences they may come to understand better what they are going through themselves. Most of all, they will learn that they are not alone.

While I have talked about the importance of routine and keeping things the same, there is one area where this can be counterproductive. When parents separate, it is important that children are exposed to the new situation as well. Keeping things the

6   Rainbows is an Irish government-funded community support programme for children and families affected by loss or death. See www.rainbowsireland.ie

same can lead a child to maintain a secret hope that their parents will get back together again. Being confronted on a regular basis with the non-resident parent's new home can help the child adapt to the reality of the situation. This secret hope that their parents will get back together is something children can cling to for many years so it is important that parents are aware of this and deal with it as gently but as firmly as possible.

Finally, it's important to focus on the future. Things will get better. You need to believe this if you want your children to believe it. You need to keep a positive outlook. While change can be difficult, it can be good. Plan nice things to look forward to and talk about the future in a positive way, acknowledging all the time that it's hard right now. Timing is important. Children need to 'wallow' a bit in the here and now before it's a good idea to introduce the positive aspects of the future. For children in the middle childhood years and especially teenagers, it's important to ask them what they think would help. They will have ideas themselves. Respect these and, if possible, take them on board. It may be that the decisions you have made with your partner are not the best ones for your children. Keep an open mind on this, taking account of your children's views and opinions, but maintaining the responsibility when it comes to making the ultimate decisions.

Remember ...

* **Know Yourself:** Your child is not you. Their feelings are their own – they have not been hurt in the same way as you have. Don't expect them to be hurt in this way and don't put this on them. They will be hurt enough themselves without having to take on your hurt as well as their own.

* **Know Your Child:** Try to anticipate how your child may be feeling and plan accordingly.

* **Listen:** Watch out for how the separation process is impacting on your child.

* **Ask:** Be proactive. Don't wait for situations to present themselves. Have regular discussions about your parenting arrangements.

* **Reassure:** Be honest, be straight, be clear and reassure. Don't make promises you can't keep. Try your best to follow through on your promises and when you simply can't, explain this to your child. Children cling to the predictability of planned events. When these fall through, it can feel to them as if their whole world is falling apart.

FOUR

Talking with Children about Death

Over my years working with children, I have always found one thing to be universally true. You never really know what's going on inside children's heads. They have such wonderful imaginations and there are so few limits to what they can conjure up in their minds. And therein lies the danger. If they don't talk about all the weird and wonderful thoughts they have going on in there, as parents we don't have the opportunity to challenge them.

Much of what I say here relates to talking with children about dying, as well as about when someone has died. A general rule is that it's better to talk about these issues than not. We can think that we are protecting our children by not talking about such difficult issues with them, believing that they are better off. However, if we believe this we are not giving children credit for their intuition and their resilience. Children know when something is not right in their family without needing to be told about it. They can pick up on the general unease around them. Which is better for them – to know the reason for this unease or to be left wondering what the cause of it is? Children are better able to cope with difficult life events than we think. Often, we can learn from them.

Know Yourself

When someone is ill and dying or when they die, everyone reacts in their own unique way. As a parent, you not only have to cope with your own feelings, you also have to look after your child through this process. Children will need even more tenderness and attention at these times, and you may find yourself compromised in terms of your ability to be there for them. Your own pain in facing up to the reality of what's happening in your life can prevent you from being able to talk about these difficult experiences. It is important to recognise this and not to beat yourself up about it. As I mentioned in chapter two, if you feel you are not up to the job, rely on others to help you out and make sure someone else is available to fill in for you. For most people, this will be a temporary arrangement. So the first step is looking after yourself. I'm reminded of the instructions on aeroplanes – make sure your own oxygen mask is securely in place before fixing your child's. You are not much help to your child if you are not steady and secure in yourself first. So finding someone to talk to about your own grief, taking the space to do whatever you need to do – to cry, to take time to reflect, or whatever it is that works for you.

If someone close to you is dying, you may find yourself gripped with panic and grief at unexpected times. You may need to decide which is better – to explain to your child why you are upset or to leave them worrying about you in the absence of information. If you decide it is best not to tell them, you will need to be able to contain your own grief and anxiety so that they are not exposed to this. Children are very sensitive to how their parents feel so it can be quite difficult to hide our feelings from them when we are upset. But at times it is necessary in order to help them manage.

Sometimes parents think that it's not okay to be emotional in front of their children for fear of causing upset. There is some wisdom in this but also some folly. Our children learn from us how to be, what to do and even how to feel. They learn this much more from observing us than from listening to what we tell them. If we can show them that it is okay to be upset when you're feeling sad, that we can do this without falling apart, without the world ending, we are teaching them an important lesson about how to deal with our emotions. If your child comes into the room and you've been upset, it can be a good thing to simply say: I was thinking about how sad it is that Dad is in hospital; Oh, I was just thinking about Granddad. I really miss him. I feel so sad that I won't be seeing him again. For children who find it difficult to express their feelings or to put words on them, it can be helpful if their parents do this for themselves. Parents are setting a good example in this way and it may open up an opportunity for a conversation about how your child feels about losing his grandparent. The important point is that the parent is able to show their upset but also able to contain it. If a parent in this scenario feels so upset that they are not able to stop crying or if by talking to their child about it they feel even more upset, then it's best not to do this. You do not want to create a situation where your child ends up consoling you, being your support. This will give two messages: a) This is too much. I am not able to cope with it. So therefore, you shouldn't get upset about it either because you won't be able to cope; and b) I am not strong enough to be here for you as your parent. You can't come to me for help because I am not able to help you.

It's important to bear in mind that just because you feel a certain way it doesn't mean others feel the same. Being aware of how you feel yourself, and being able to talk to your friends or partner about this will help you know how you feel. This way, you will be better able to give your child the space they need to feel their own feelings, to have their own thoughts that may or may not be different from yours. You don't want your children to feel there is some 'right' way to feel. You want them to be allowed to feel whatever they feel and to be able to say this if they need to. And you don't want your child to feel they have to mind you. You're the adult, you're the parent; it's your job to mind them, not theirs to mind you.

Know Your Child
A parent I know describes her two boys like this: one meets the world with 'yes', the other with 'no'. The older child was born

hungry; he greedily devoured his feeds, he didn't sleep during the day, preferring to sit and watch all that was going on around him. The younger child took long naps, was a much heavier baby and didn't seem to need to feed so much. As he grew, the older boy was characterised as a child who loved new activities, wanting to try new experiences, always interested in what was different. The younger boy was more cautious about new experiences. He preferred the comfort zone of what was familiar. His first instinct was to reject the new, until he felt comfortable enough in himself to engage. The older boy launched himself right into new experiences.

Our personalities were developing from the time we were in the womb. Mothers describe an 'active' or a 'quiet' baby in the womb and observe that this trait continues after birth. Children have different personalities and engage with the world in various ways depending on their temperament or personality. Thus, children respond to difficult life events differently and need appropriate responses from those who care for them. An inward-looking 'introvert' child may need some time to himself while a more outward-looking 'extrovert' child may need more stimulation through conversation or peer play activities. Occasionally over the years I have met parents who told me I treated them all the same when referring to how they parented their children. First, I found this hard to believe. How can you treat children the same when they are so different? This doesn't allow for the fact that children themselves bring something to the interactions we have with them. We respond differently to different children partly because they evoke a different response in us and because they respond differently to us. Second, if this were indeed possible, would it be fair not to take account of the individual child, with their individual needs? Surely one child might benefit from this approach while another child's needs might go completely unmet?

Different children will experience different anxieties about impending death or death itself. If, as a parent, you are having a conversation about someone who is dying, each child will have different worries or questions. It can be very difficult for a parent to anticipate these questions because children have such wonderful and creative imaginations. Being open to each child's uniqueness will help. Expect the unexpected. Children may ask questions such as: what happens to the person after they die? Where do they go? If children have been to funerals that involved burials in graveyards, they may have questions about the coffin and the grave – questions that are difficult to answer and ones that you 'as a parent' may feel uncomfortable thinking about while you deal with your own grief. Your own religious beliefs may bring some assistance in dealing with these questions, as the answers may vary depending on such beliefs. The important point is to encourage the questions as this will give you an insight into how your child is coping with their own grief.

Each child is unique and will react to experiences such as death in their own way. How has your child reacted to loss or separation in the past? Do they engage with their feelings about this, allowing themselves to feel the pain? Or do they avoid it, pretend it's not happening, distract themselves and thus avoid unpleasant feelings? Probably the best way to deal with loss is by adopting a little bit of both. It is important to be able to learn to tolerate the pain of loss – to be able to give away that toy that hasn't been seen or played with for a long time; to be able to grieve the loss of a babysitter or childminder; to be able to say goodbye and be open to new experiences. What does your child do to help them cope with such experiences? The 'blankie' or 'soother' helps the baby develop the skill of self-soothing. We all need our 'blankie' – it just takes on a different form as we get older.

Younger children may need lots of physical comfort – cuddles and holding. For children who don't like too much physical contact, it may be a case of simply sitting with them, making sure they know you are near, and are there if they need you. Older children, depending on whether they like to talk about their feelings or not, may need to talk or may need you to say the things they need to hear.

Listen

When a child has experienced a loss, be that the loss of a pet or a friend moving away, she will have her own unique feelings about this. It's important as I mentioned earlier that we don't assume we know what it feels like for them. We are probably thinking about what we would feel like if this happened to us. But our children are not us. He is his own person with his own unique personality; she is her own person with her own distinctive feelings that are all her own. We therefore have to listen to our children if we want to know how they are feeling. Listening involves most of all watching. Noticing the little changes in patterns, noticing the moods, noticing the quietness or the irritability or the anger. Very young children tell us how they are feeling through their behaviour. This is the way they communicate that all is not well.

We need to be able to notice the behaviour and understand that this is a form of communication. What children do not need is to be punished for making it known that all is not okay in their world. They do not need our irritation, our intolerance or our expectation that they behave appropriately regardless of how they are feeling. What they need is our understanding, our ability to see beyond what is in front of our noses and to be able to read the signals that they are trying to send us, however clumsy a means of communication that might seem to us to be. Hearing how they feel about the small losses they experience helps us to understand more how they might feel about the big ones. Moving class can mean losing a teacher that your child was fond of. How do they talk about this? How do they express how this experience is for them? How do they manage this loss? Do they deal with it by ignoring it and not talking about it at all? This might be your cue to ask them about it, to bring it up in conversation, to acknowledge that sometimes it can be hard to lose a teacher that you have become fond of, that knows and understands you.

Another experience to watch out for that helps reflect how your child deals with loss in general is that of losing friends. If friends move away or if there is less contact because of a divergence of interests, or if they simply fall out, this can be a good opportunity to encourage your child to learn to grieve and mourn. If your child talks about missing their friend, the instinctive response from some parents can be to distract them or to focus their attention elsewhere, perhaps on another friendship. It can be easy to miss out on this opportunity to help your child deal with grief. Watching out for these opportunities will help you to help your child make sense of these experiences, talk about their feelings and by doing so, help them to mourn the loss and move on.

Children may have questions: why did she die? Where is she now? You may need to explain what death means to younger children who have no experience of death. You may need to explain how the body works and how it stops working when we die.

When children want to know what happens to people after they die, these questions bring up issues to do with faith beliefs and also may trigger questions that parents have not given much thought to themselves. As a mother of teenage boys, I am constantly bombarded with questions. They want to know what I think about this and that. Often I haven't given the matter a lot of thought at all.

This is a common experience for parents – to be absolutely flummoxed by a question. Like a rabbit caught in a headlight. And panic sets in. What on earth do I say? If you find yourself caught in a situation like this, it's important not to feel ambushed into saying something that you will later need to renege on. Give yourself time: oh gosh, that's a good question. I'll need to think about that a bit. I'm not sure how to answer that one could come in useful as a ready-made response. You want to be honest, you want to be straight and you don't want to make things worse. As a bonus, you could make things better.

Listening, then, regardless of the age of your child, involves watching out for signs that they are trying to communicate their feelings and also watching out for when they are trying to talk about how they feel. With primary school children, it can be very useful to eavesdrop on conversations children have with their friends. I have found invaluable those times when I was driving children home from school and listened in to the chat between them and their friends about what happened in the schoolyard that day. This can be a great way of picking up information that they might find difficult to relay to you directly.

Ask

Observing your child will give you the opportunity to ask them about how they are feeling. A good way to begin the process of asking is simply to comment on their behaviour. This way, you are giving them the message that you have noticed, that you care about how they are, and that you are here to listen if they choose to speak with you. Children need so much to be noticed, no matter what age they are. When they are older, they may not 'want' to be noticed but they do need to be noticed. This need doesn't change whether as a baby, a toddler, an older child, a teenager or an adult. It is how we show each other that we care: we notice.

Asking questions out of the blue will most likely receive a blank response. Children need help to know what you are talking about if you ask them questions about how they are feeling. They need what we call 'anchors'. You need to lead into a conversation so that they know what you are talking about. Asking them 'how are you feeling?' will probably get a 'fine' in reply. However, start talking about the person that died, followed by a question about whether they think about them and they may give you much more information. This in turn can help the child reflect on how they feel and then they might be able to share this with you. Or, as I mentioned above, talk about how you're feeling and then turn the conversation to them and ask them how they feel.

With younger children in particular, it is important to find opportunities to have conversations about death. I often think that children who grow up on farms are fortunate in being exposed to the life cycle in a way that is not so threatening for them as it is if their first experience of death is of a loved one. The normality of animals being born and dying helps children to understand life and death as there are opportunities for conversations about such issues. These experiences may trigger questions for them – questions that need to be voiced out loud. The answers can help them to process grief when the time comes for them to experience it in their family or social network.

Creating a climate within a family where children feel free to ask questions helps at times like these. If children are accustomed to being asked questions from an early age, they are more likely to consider it okay to be the one asking the questions. Sometimes parents are busy, preoccupied or don't quite know how to respond to these questions. If this happens, it's a good idea to promise to come back to them when you do have time to chat. This way, you encourage the questions. You keep the channels of communication open. You teach them that it's good to ask questions.

When someone is terminally ill, whether and how much to tell your children will really depend on the individual circumstances. There are no hard and fast rules about it, although children tend to do better when they have been prepared in some ways for death. Preparation time gives them an opportunity to ask questions they may have or help them make sense of it all. It also means that, depending on how much time there is, the process of loss and grieving can be a more gradual process. It is more difficult for children and adults to deal with grief when a death has been sudden and unexpected. When someone is ill and is expected to die, this is an opportunity to have conversations about the matter before your child has to deal with the reality of death. Younger children often do not understand the irreversibility of death. They don't see it as something permanent – as with their belief in magic, they may still hold on to the belief that the person may get better or that even when they die, they might come back again next week. Because of this, it can be less upsetting for them to have conversations about someone dying and more upsetting for the adult speaking with them.

Older children may feel resentful afterwards when they discover that people knew the person was going to die and didn't say so. They may have wanted to say things to the person. Or they may simply need time to adjust to the reality of death and knowing about it in advance, when this is possible, helps them along this path. As with all other difficult information, and as discussed in the earlier chapter on talking with children about separation, it's best to give clear concrete information in stages, depending on how your child reacts to and deals with such information.

Reassure

Many researchers and experts have written about the process of grief and the typical stages that people go through when grieving a loved one. Elisabeth Kübler-Ross[7] described five stages of grieving in adults: denial, anger, bargaining, depression and acceptance; while John Bowlby[8] likened grief in children to coping with separation and described the following stages of the grieving process: shock, searching, depression and reorganisation or recovery. These stages can be applied to all losses, not just the death of someone close. These writings are helpful because they are based on large numbers of people and so we get a sense of the typical patterns of how people grieve. They can also be unhelpful if we expect each individual to conform to this pattern. As with any research done with large numbers, it is the typical pattern that is identified. This may or may not apply to each individual. And so it may or may not apply to you or to your child. More recent literature[9] emphasises the importance

---

7   E. Kübler-Ross, *On Death and Dying* (New York: Macmillan, 1969).

8   J. Bowlby, *Attachment and Loss*, Vol. 3, Loss (London: Hogarth Press, 1980).

9   M. Dowling, *Exploring the experiences of bereavement and counselling among young people who are bereaved*, unpublished doctoral dissertation (Dublin: Dublin City University, 2014).

of maintaining the bond with the person who has died, which is not taken account of in these 'stage' models of the grieving process. Keeping the memory of the lost one alive – looking at pictures, telling stories about them, are considered important in helping us cope with the death of a loved one.

We know that it is normal to be upset when someone dies; it is normal to be angry; it is normal to want to obsess about the person and talk about little else; it is normal to want to visit a grave over and over for a time after the person dies; it is normal to storm and rage against the person for leaving us, for abandoning us. This is reassuring for us to know that we are not going mad, it is simply part of the process of grieving. And we also know that with time, and support, this will pass. The pain will become somewhat less intense. The urge to talk about the person all the time, to look over the photographs day in day out, diminishes. We may still need to do these things but will no longer experience these urges to the same degree. The feelings may never go away but they will ease over time. Things will get better.

Children often need reassurance that it is okay to feel as they do, and that the feelings will become less painful over time. Younger children don't have as much life experience to draw on to know this and so are more dependent on their parents to instil this belief in them. It may feel to them like it will never get better, that they are always going to feel this lost, this desperate, this fearful. Of course, it is essential that you believe things will improve yourself. Children will sense if you don't believe it. They will see through your platitudes and your kind words to how you really feel. You must lead by example. If you believe it, you will be giving them permission to believe it. After all, to believe that things will get better can sometimes feel like a betrayal of the loved one who is dying or who has died. We can go on without you. We will be okay. It can feel like a questioning of the love that is felt for that person. If I really loved him, I could never feel better.

When someone close to a child is dying, it is helpful for most children to be able to talk about it. This is part of the process of grieving: to prepare for the death. The manner in which the dying person is dealing with the impending death will, of course, strongly influence how these conversations go. If a person has accepted the inevitability of the death and is able to talk about it, to reminisce and acknowledge the sadness that comes with their passing, this can greatly help those of us who get left behind. We can have conversations that help us adjust to the pain of the loss we are about to experience.

Some children may find such conversations just too painful. Their way of coping with it may be to pretend it isn't happening, to pretend they didn't understand when you tried to explain events to them. It's probably better to allow them to keep up this pretence and not challenge them, but it's not a good idea for you to also pretend it isn't happening. Finding opportunities to mention the fact that the person may not be around for future events can be a gentle way of reminding the child of something that they are not really able to let in but nevertheless will need to face up to eventually.

It is often helpful to reassure a child by telling them that the person who died would not have wanted them to continue to feel so sad. Remind them of how that person was in life. Share stories about your life together that your child may not be aware of. Look back over photographs so that you and your child can keep the memories alive. Remind your child (and yourself) that the person who died would want them to get on with their lives and enjoy themselves. Encourage them to go off with their friends, to engage with their routine activities, to do things that give them some pleasure. Reassure them that to forget about the loved one from time to time is normal and healthy and that there is no need to feel guilty about this.

I often think that there is nothing more reassuring at funerals than to see children running around having a good time. For a time, the sadness is forgotten and play takes over. We can learn a lot from our children at times like these.

Remember ...

* **Know Yourself:** Take your own space to grieve or prepare for the death of a loved one. Teach your child about grieving through example.

* **Know Your Child:** Expect the unexpected. Don't assume that they are feeling the same way as you are – give them space to have their own reactions.

* **Listen:** Watch your child closely for indicators of how they are coping with grief. Allow them to have fun and enjoy their being able to do this.

* **Ask:** Encourage conversation tentatively and gently if this is all your child is able for, but be mindful of those situations in which it is you who is not able for it. Talk about the person who has died and keep their memory alive.

* **Reassure:** Reassure your child that it is okay to be upset, it is okay to be angry, it is okay to forget about their grief for a time – whatever they feel, it is okay. Feelings are not 'right' or 'wrong', they just are.

FIVE

Talking with Children about Bullying

Bullying has become a universally recognised phenomenon to the point that it is standard practice for schools to have a policy on the subject. In Ireland, such policies describe bullying as 'repeated aggression, verbal, psychological or physical, conducted by an individual or groups against others'.[10]

In Ireland, the My World survey published by the School of Psychology, University College Dublin and Headstrong, the national organisation for youth mental health in Ireland, showed that 40 per cent of adolescents surveyed had experienced bullying at some point in time.[11]

The issue of bullying is one for all parents. Your child may not bully another child or be directly bullied but for every child who has been bullied or who bullies, a large number of other children witness it. Some of these children support the bullying behaviour by not doing anything. Research on bullying shows that peer groups are very important in dealing with bullying behaviour.[12] Some children want to do something to help the child being bullied but don't know how to help or may fear consequences for themselves if they support the victim. Some children believe that it's best to

---

10 M. O'Moore, and S. J. Minton, *Dealing with Bullying in Schools: A Training Manual for Teachers, Parents and Other Professionals* (London: Paul Chapman Publishing, 2004).

11 See http://researchrepository.ucd.ie/bitstream/handle/10197/4286/My_World_ Survey_2012_Online%284%29.pdf?sequence=1

12 K. Rigby, *How Parents and Educators can Reduce Bullying at School* (Victoria, Australia: Blackwell Publishing, 2008).

simply ignore the bullying, in the belief that by not paying attention to it that it will stop.

Much research has been done in this area and we know more nowadays about the negative impact that certain responses can have on children who bully and children who are bullied. We know that it is a serious issue that deserves a lot of attention from both parents and schools and that there can be both short-term and long-term negative psychological consequence for children involved.

Know Yourself

Bullying is so common that many parents will have experienced such incidents themselves as a child or indeed in adulthood. These experiences can leave emotional scars that are reactivated when we are faced with our children having similar experiences. If we have not 'dealt with' our own experiences, that is, if we have not reflected on them sufficiently and been able to move on in such a way that we are not as affected by them, then they can continue to impact on us in terms of how we address the issue with our children. We may interpret behaviour as bullying when we see interactions between children that are not in fact bullying but horseplay or ordinary peer conflicts. We may overlook incidents of bullying because our anxiety about dealing with it blinds us to its reality.

When children are particularly vulnerable to being bullied, much of what is needed is improved social skills – in particular, learning to be assertive (as opposed to aggressive). Children first learn these skills in the home. It is difficult for a parent to teach their child to be assertive if the parent is lacking in these skills themselves. Many children see a parent or older sibling being bullied in the home. Older siblings can be very astute at getting their own way, at bullying their younger siblings. If this is not addressed appropriately, it is extremely difficult for a child to learn how to behave assertively in their peer group. Children respond differently to growing up in a home where there is violence or bullying. Some children who may be timid, shy or unassertive may find it difficult to stand up to inappropriate behaviour from their peers. They may be more likely to be a target of bullying behaviour outside the home. Other children may act out this aggression, imitating what they see at home, and may be more likely to bully others. In both cases, these children have not learned appropriate assertive behaviour: how to relate to others in a way that they respect themselves and respect others. If your child describes an incident at school that upset them, you may have a number of reactions. You may view the incident as just that – incidental. Wanting to give other children the benefit of the doubt, you may feel that your child overreacted, or that the behaviour wasn't intentional. You may also be reluctant to entertain the possibility that your child is being targeted for negative attention – this is not easy for many parents to acknowledge. You may yourself overreact, and interpret an incident as targeted bullying when in fact it was just a random incident and your child was unfortunate to get caught up in something that wasn't about them at all. Parents, for the most part, are particularly sensitive to any hurt that may be directed at their child. Part of being protective is being sensitive to the possibility of harm coming to your child. It can be difficult to separate out what is intentional and what is not when you are relying on your child's account of what happened. Even if you observed the incident, it may be difficult to discern bullying as it can be very subtle and difficult to recognise, particularly in the early stages.

You may feel reluctant to bring the incident to the attention of the school, out of fear that you are drawing unwanted attention to your child or that you will be seen as overreacting or an interfering parent. Or you may feel very angry that the school has allowed such an incident to take place and want to storm into the school to complain. You may feel very angry towards the child or children involved in the bullying incident. It can be easy to lose sight of the fact that this is another child and that if they are engaging in bullying behaviour, there is something not right in their world. If a child is happy and content, they won't feel the need to inflict hurt on others.

Each school has an anti-bullying policy that draws on general principles agreed at a national level. It is important for parents to examine these policies and learn about the steps to take if they are concerned their child is being bullied and how the school responds to such behaviour. It is your responsibility to alert the school to the concerns you have, and it is the school's responsibility to deal with the matter, with your cooperation. The school's methods for dealing with bullying may appear questionable to you. You may need to learn more about what the school policy and procedures are based upon before you judge them to be adequate for your situation. This is a difficult issue for schools to deal with and schools throughout Europe have had varying success with different types of interventions for dealing with bullying.[13] However, schools need your cooperation if they are to be successful in dealing with the issue for your child.

While it is difficult to discover that your child is being bullied it can be even more difficult to discover that your child is bullying another child. If parents of children who are engaged in bullying behaviour cannot accept that this is happening, it is extremely difficult for the child concerned to be able to deal with it and to understand the underlying meaning of the bullying behaviour for them. They will not be able to get their needs met if their parents are not able to face up to the facts. Extreme reactions such as denying that such a thing could be happening or, at the other end of the spectrum, showing your child how horrified you are at their behaviour, is not helpful. Children who engage in bullying need help. They need to be loved and understood, they need their behaviour to be understood. In general, it is accepted that a 'no-blame' approach is more effective in dealing with bullying behaviour. As a parent, it is important that you take your child's side and let them know that you are there for them and will help them through this. As I've

---

13 P. Smith, D. Pepler, and K. Rigby, *Bullying in Schools: How Successful Can Interventions Be?* (Cambridge: Cambridge University Press, 2004).

mentioned previously, this does not mean colluding with them in denying their culpability, nor does it mean punishing them severely for their behaviour. Rather, it is about warmth and firmness. As mentioned, the school will have a policy and a set of procedures for dealing with the issue. As parents, it is essential to work with the school to follow any guidance offered and to give your child a clear message that you are working together with teachers to help your child overcome these difficulties.

Know Your Child
Some children, by virtue of their personalities, do not fit in with the crowd. They are a little different from their peers – it may be that they are quiet or that they are boisterous; it may be that they are particularly tall or particularly small for their age; it may be that their interests are out of sync with other children of the same age; it may be that they are good at school or falling behind with their schoolwork; it may be that other children perceive them as not being able to stand up for themselves; it may be that they tend to show off in front of others; it may be that they don't have many friends. Teaching children that it is okay to be different can help them accept themselves as they are. If children are content in their own uniqueness, they are less likely to be targeted by others for being different. If they are teased for being different, they will not experience this as hurtful because they are comfortable in their own skin. Those who are teasing them will not get the reaction they desire. There will be no reinforcement for them to continue their teasing. If a child sees their own uniqueness as a strength rather than a weakness, then other children will be more inclined to see this as a strength too.

Life experiences have their impact on us all. Disruptions in the family and difficulty with managing transitions can bring more stress on a family and in turn on individual children. Children may go through difficult times when they are more susceptible to being bullied. Knowing your child and how he or she reacts to changes in family circumstances can help you to anticipate when they may be having a difficult time and to plan accordingly. You may need to keep a closer eye on them and their peer relationships during such transitions. Watching the power relationships within peer groups will give you some idea of how they get played out in a group of children or even when your child is playing or interacting with one other friend. What role does your child play in this? What role does his or her friend play? Is your child always inclined to go along with what the other child wants? Is this out of politeness or submissiveness? Is your child inclined to dominate other children in their play or interactions? Does this happen with some children and not others?

Unfortunately, children who tend to be targeted for bullying are also the children who may be less inclined to tell someone about it. Their shyness or passivity inhibits them from first being able to stand up for themselves in the face of bullying, and also inhibits them from telling a teacher or a parent about what is going on. Such children therefore need more help in being able to speak out when something is wrong.

Children often do not have an appreciation of the power they hold over younger children. They therefore need to be taught to take responsibility for the fact that they are older, that concessions must be made when they are playing with younger children. Sometimes it is necessary to point out the fact that the younger child is not as physically strong as their older playmate or sibling and therefore the older child needs to take this into account, or that because they are younger, they are not as good at thinking their way out of situations. The parent needs to be very clear that this is just because they are younger, as the last thing a parent wants to do is to undermine this child even further.

Be open to the possibility that your child may be involved in bullying at some point, and use this knowledge to inform how you talk with your child about bullying. It is useful to think about what your reaction would be if they were to tell you about bullying they are experiencing. They may be afraid that you will cut back on the little bit of independence they have, that you will not allow them out with their friends, or that you will tell the teachers and they will be known as a 'rat'. If the bullying is happening online, they may fear that your response will be to take their mobile phone, computer or limit internet access.

Listen

The psychological impact of bullying can be seen in its short-term forms and in its long-term forms. As with other traumatic life experiences, children in the short term can experience difficulties with eating, sleeping, mood and anxiety. They can lose interest in food or 'comfort eat', resulting in weight loss or gain. They can have difficulties sleeping or they can oversleep, resulting in difficulties getting up for school and in concentrating in class. They can struggle more with homework, partly due to these concentration problems but also due to a lack of motivation or lack of belief in themselves and their abilities. Bullying has a significant impact on a child's self-esteem, how they feel about themselves, the value they place on themselves. Watching out for how a child feels about himself or herself can help you as a parent to get a sense of whether something of this nature is going on.

If the bullying is happening in school, they can be reluctant to attend, claiming to be sick and wanting to stay home. They can suffer from psychosomatic complaints such as regular headaches or tummy aches. Any changes in their behaviour can be a sign that something is not right. Watching out for such changes and noticing them if they do occur is an important first step for a parent in recognising the short-term effects of bullying. It may be necessary for you to comment on changes you have noticed and use this as an opportunity to ask your child about school and their relationships with other children. Keeping in mind the possibility that your child may be bullied will help you notice any signs that could suggest this. Listening to how your child describes their interactions with others can help you think about what questions you may need to ask.

Children will often give misleading information to try to cover up what is happening to them. They may give explanations for a torn schoolbag, a cut on the leg, a bruise on the arm or bouts of tearfulness, that don't add up. If you think this is what's happening, it's probably best not to confront the child and insist on the truth. It may be useful to let them know in some way that you are not convinced by their story. However, they are covering up for a reason. It's important to understand what the reason might be before you push for details that they may not be ready to give you. They may be feeling ashamed that they are not able to deal with the situation themselves. They may need reassurance before they feel comfortable to speak out.

If you are really unsure as to whether something of this nature is going on in school, it can be useful to change your routine so that you have more opportunities to observe your child interacting with other children in the school. This may involve collecting your child from school now and again if they usually travel independently; volunteering to help out with school events such as school trips or fundraising projects; asking teachers how your child is getting on with their peers; or expressing your concern to your child's teacher and asking them to be vigilant when they are interacting with their peers.

Having an ongoing relationship with a school teacher can be very helpful in that you then have another source of information to draw on. In primary schools, teachers are well placed to see how children interact with their peers. They will know more about how your child interacts with other children in the class and they will know the other children about whom you may have concerns. Maintaining an open channel of communication with a teacher ensures that you don't have to wait until a problem develops before discussing it. You can have ongoing conversations, noting your concerns about your child's behaviour and asking if there is anything going on in school that might help to explain this behaviour. If you are concerned that your child is being bullied, it's important to alert the school as early as possible so that they can also watch out for any evidence of this. Most schools, in my experience, will welcome this open communication.

Putting a stop to the bullying is the first step in preventing the long-term effects. Many adults who attend counselling and psychotherapy in adulthood describe bullying experiences they had in school that affected their self-esteem. Some adults find that experiences of depression or anxiety can be traced back to feelings they have about bullying experiences as a child. The long-term impact of bullying can manifest itself in the broad range of psychological difficulties that can stem from difficult life experiences – depression, anxiety, eating disorders, relationship difficulties and substance abuse. The experience may also impact on people's relationships with colleagues in adulthood in that they find themselves in similar situations in the workplace. Bullying in the workplace is just as big a problem as bullying in schools. Dealing with the short-term impact can, to some extent, help individuals avoid such experiences in the future.

Ask

As with the other issues I have discussed in this book, creating an atmosphere where we can talk with children and encourage them to talk with us about troublesome life experiences begins in the home. If, as a parent, you suspect that an older sibling is picking on a younger sibling, it is important to speak with both children separately. Observing the behaviour is of course ideal – if you have seen something happening, you can use this information in addressing the conflict. Asking a younger child about something that just happened in front of their older siblings is unlikely to reveal bullying behaviour. The younger child may have been threatened not to tell. Speaking to each child separately and listening carefully to their side of the story encourages children to talk about such experiences openly.

Dealing with incidents such as these in the immediate aftermath tends to be more effective. Neither child has had too much time to feel the impact of the interaction. Neither have they had too much time to come up with a misleading explanation.

These situations are more manageable when the behaviour is between siblings as you do not need to rely on other adults to cooperate with you. When the bullying is happening between friends or when neighbouring children are involved, you are very dependant on the parents of the other children involved. Your relationship with those parents will be pivotal in this conversation. How you approach the conversation will have a significant impact on their willingness to engage with you. If you appear to be blaming their child, they may be reluctant to take on board your concerns. It is therefore important that, particularly with younger children, you engage in regular ongoing conversations with the parents of the children your child interacts with. Doing so will make it easier to talk cordially in the event that more difficult conversations are needed. Asking other parents how they think your children are interacting can help draw other parents' attention to the children's play and perhaps help them notice when things are not going so well. Being open to their concerns and being honest about your child and how he or she interacts with others will also help them to acknowledge how their own child is behaving. Communicating that you care about their child and have their interests at heart goes a long way in helping other parents see the situation from your point of view.

If you are trying to initiate a conversation with your child about bullying in general, it can be helpful to mention another situation of bullying – perhaps a friend has told you that their child experienced bullying; perhaps you experienced this yourself in school. By raising the topic, you are inviting your child to talk about the issue in general. This might provide an opening for them to tell you if something is happening to them. It might also provide an opening for you to ask them if they have ever had any experiences at school that might be called bullying.

If you suspect that your child is involved in a bullying incident, either as the child being bullied or the child who is doing the bullying, it's usually best not to ask directly about this in the first instance, given how reluctant children are to talk. Firstly, it can be difficult for children to understand that they are being bullied. They may know that what is happening is making them feel very uncomfortable or that they are upset about it, but they may not see it as bullying. They may be reluctant to see themselves in this light – as a 'victim' of 'bullying'. This may feel like an added failure to them, on top of not being able to manage the situation. They may not want to 'make a big deal of it', concerned that this will bring unwanted attention on them and simply make them feel worse. As previously noted, noticing how your child is behaving can help you find an opportunity to have a conversation about their well-being. Commenting on what you have noticed can give them an opening to talk about what is bothering them. Having regular conversations like this can help you both lead into a conversation that may be more difficult for them. They may need to test the waters with you before deciding to tell you the details. They may need to feel more secure in themselves, or more secure in their relationship with you, before they are comfortable enough to share this difficult information.

Reassure
One of the most positive characteristics that children can have in terms of their overall well-being is that of self-esteem and self-efficacy. Promoting good self-esteem and self-efficacy in our children gives them the skills they need to deal with the adversities they experience as they go through life. Showing children we care

about them, that we admire their achievements, that we respect their individuality, that we enjoy spending time with them all helps bolster their self-esteem. Giving our children opportunities to succeed, to develop their independence and engage in activities that they are good at helps promote a sense of themselves as effective human beings.

Teaching our children how to be assertive in their sibling and peer relationships gives them a good grounding during times when they have to deal with conflict and we are not around to help them. Advising them on how to deal with minor peer conflicts and praising them for the times they successfully deal with these situations helps them develop a sense of social competence that will be of great benefit if they find themselves on the receiving end of persistent or persecutory negative attention from peers.

If your child does tell you about being bullied, the first response they need is a sympathetic one. Although a parent's instinct may be to minimise the gravity of the situation in the belief that the child needs to develop a way of taking things in his or her stride, this reaction can lead to your child feeling unheard, misunderstood, undervalued and uncared for. It can also deter them from mentioning any similar incidents again. Conversely, the parent may overreact. This can lead to your child attempting to minimise it, to downplay the incident out of fear that you will do something drastic. The best approach is to listen patiently and attentively, following the lead your child gives you, sympathising where they appear to be looking for sympathy, agreeing with the possible explanations they themselves are coming up with, and making gentle suggestions as to other possibilities.

It is understandable that parents want to get as much detail as possible: what happened? Who was involved? When did it happen? Who else was there? Did anyone do anything to help? However, it's important not to bombard your child with questions and make them feel they are being interrogated. Firstly, they need reassurance, sympathy and support. They need to be told that they were right to tell you and that you will help them sort this out.

It's important to adopt a collaborative approach and to find a solution together. This way you are giving the message that you are not going to take things out of their hands completely. If you do, you could undermine your child even further, reinforcing the message that they probably received through the bullying behaviour, that is, that they are weak. It's important to see the problem as something to be overcome, to instil in your child confidence that this will be resolved (even if you don't feel convinced yourself) and that action needs to be taken as a first step towards resolution. It is often the case that by the time your child has told you about the bullying, they have tried to solve the problem themselves and failed. It is a good idea to get some details of these attempts before you offer some suggestions yourself. It is therefore really important that you re-awaken some hope for them in being able to tackle the problem. If you make suggestions that they have already tried themselves, it can be easy for them to respond: I did that. It didn't work. However, taking charge of the situation, particularly for younger children, can bring a sense of relief to your child. It's important that they realise that now that you know about what is happening, you will be doing something about it.

Remember ...

* **Know Your Child:** Be aware of your children's vulnerabilities and what may place them at risk of being involved in bullying and what may prevent them from telling you about it if they are bullied.

* **Listen:** Listen to your child talking about his or her interactions with peers. Use these conversations as opportunities to get a sense of the power relationships in these groups of peers. Watch out for changes in behaviour that may be a sign that your child is involved in bullying.

* **Ask:** Ask your child about his or her peer relationships. Ask your child about his or her views on bullying. Use school prevention programmes as an opportunity to have these conversations.

* **Reassure:** Reassure your children that they are right to tell you about the bullying. Be sympathetic in your response. Impress upon them the fact that now that you know about it, you will be taking action to resolve the issue.

SIX

Talking about Sexual Abuse

Children are very vulnerable at any age when it comes to sexual abuse, but younger children are particularly so for a number of reasons. They will not understand what is happening and have no words to describe it. As children grow older and come to understand more about sex they will often remember what happened to them at an early age and may come to feel very ashamed. Having kept the secret already, they may find it difficult to speak out about it now. Unfortunately, even when children either don't remember abuse that happened at an early age or have very hazy memories of it, the impact of this experience can be felt many years later. Older children will probably have a good idea about what the sexual abuse means. They know that it is wrong and that it shouldn't be happening. They know that it makes them feel uncomfortable. However, they also may understand the consequences of speaking out. They know that it will cause trouble, maybe even family breakdown. This can stop them from getting the help that they need.

Having an experience of sexual abuse in childhood can have a significant impact on how children develop. Children can feel 'different' and 'bad inside' because of what happened and this can isolate them from other children. It can affect their self-esteem and their ability to socialise with other children, to make friends and thus gain all the benefits that friendship brings to a child's life. It can interfere with their school work as they may have difficulties concentrating in class. Shame is a very insidious emotion. It is difficult to shift and it can wreak havoc with people's intimate relationships in adulthood. Unfortunately, many children who have been sexually abused feel ashamed about what happened, are unable to talk to someone about it and thus are prevented from getting much needed help in order to overcome that shame. Children who have been sexually abused are at a higher risk of sexual exploitation in adulthood. They are also at a higher risk of developing a range of psychological problems such as depression, anxiety, substance abuse and eating disorders.

Talking with children from a very early age about the need to tell you, as their parent, if anyone does anything to them that makes them feel uncomfortable is essential. Many argue that it places an unfair burden on children to teach them to protect themselves from abuse. I agree. But I have met many parents in the course of my work who it seems to me have been very protective of their children – and yet their children were sexually abused. There is only so much that parents can do to protect their children. They can supervise their children, but children need to be able to go off with their friends and spend time alone in order to develop their independence. Parents can be careful about the people who come into contact with their children, but most children are abused by someone they know – a friendly neighbour, a regular babysitter, a favourite uncle, a caring grandparent, an older sibling, a parent or parent's partner. Because sexual abuse for the most part takes place in such a secretive context – usually only two people are involved and at least one of them doesn't want anyone to know about it – the burden often falls to the child to speak out.

Helping children to understand that bad things can happen is not introducing unnecessary ideas into children's heads. It is protecting them from the reality of child sexual abuse. A national study in Ireland carried out by the Royal College of Surgeons[14] in Ireland and published in 2002 found that one in four Irish adults had an unwanted sexual experience under the age of seventeen.

14 McGee, H., Garavan, R., deBarra, M., Byrne, J. & Conroy, R. *Sexual Assault and Violence in Ireland*, (Dublin: Dublin Rape Crisis Centre, 2002) (See http://epubs. rcsi.ie/cgi/viewcontent.cgi?article=1014&context=psycholrep).

While we do not have up-to-date figures on child sexual abuse reports, there is no evidence to suggest that sexual abuse in Ireland is any less prevalent today. We can then ask: could our child be that one in four? This is sobering thought.

Although I do not go into much detail in this chapter about talking with teenagers about their own sexually harmful behaviour, it is important for parents to be aware that in the United States it is estimated that about one-third of child sexual abuse is perpetrated on children by adolescents. While it is true that most adolescents and adults who sexually abuse children have themselves been abused, it is not the case that most children who have been abused go on to abuse other children. Sometimes teenagers experiment with younger children as a way of exploring their own sexual feelings. Lack of supervision, coupled with psychological difficulties on the part of the teenager, can create opportunities for adolescents to act out sexually with younger children. If they are not 'caught' early, they can increasingly lose the ability to control their impulses and the behaviour can escalate. It is really important that these young people get help as early as possible. There are several therapy programmes available nowadays for children and young people with sexually harmful behaviour, showing promising results.

Know Yourself
Parents often worry about introducing the topic of sexual abuse to young children. They worry that introducing the topic is 'putting ideas in their heads' and thus leaves them more at risk. Time and time again, research proves this to be a false belief. Children who are better informed are better protected. As a parent, you want to establish a pattern of communication with your child from an early age which means that should anything out of the ordinary happen in their daily life, they will tell you. Parents ask: at what age should we start talking to our child about sexual abuse? I say: from the beginning. Because this is such an uncomfortable

topic to talk about, we are understandably reluctant to introduce it to our beautiful innocent children. Unfortunately, children may come into contact with others who will take advantage of their beauty and innocence, from a very young age, long before we think they are 'ready' to talk about it.

Being able to talk with children about sexual abuse requires being comfortable in yourself when having these conversations. The National Society for the Prevention of Cruelty to Children (NSPCC) has some excellent resources on their website (www.nspcc. org.uh) to help parents prepare for such conversations. If you feel squeamish about having the conversation, your child will pick this up from you and be left with the message that it's not okay to talk about this subject. This will not help them come to you if they have a question or a worry. So it's good to be able to talk to someone about it before you broach the subject with your child. Different people will have different views about whether it is a good idea to be having these conversations so you will need to talk to someone who you know will be supportive. Talking through your own anxieties about having the conversation will help you prepare for it better. If you feel ill-equipped to have these conversations, think how ill-equipped your son or daughter will be in having to deal with the reality.

When talking about sexual abuse there are two particular problems parents may have in introducing this topic. If you have had an experience of sexual abuse in your own childhood, you may want to avoid the topic altogether or you may 'overdo' it. You may have coped with your own experiences by avoiding thinking about them and avoiding talking about them. However, while this can be an understandable strategy to use, people often find that it only lasts so long. When they have their own children, particularly when those children reach the age when the parent was abused, these strategies tend to break down. Refusing to face up to one's own pain can leave us blind to the risks facing our children. An example of this is the young woman who left her baby daughter with her parents while she went to work each day. The fact that her father abused her many years beforehand was never spoken of in the family. The woman didn't even think of it much anymore. She could not conceive that she might be leaving her daughter at risk. Her beautiful daughter? He could never abuse her, surely? Part of the problem here is that the young woman never spoke about the abuse. She blamed herself for what happened. In blaming herself, she took responsibility for the abuse rather than placing it where it belonged – with her father. She therefore didn't see that her father had a problem – until he abused her daughter. When she then spoke out about her own experience of abuse, she was castigated. Those who believed her were astonished. How could she leave her daughter with a man she knew to be a sex abuser? Those who did not believe her used the same logic – the fact that she would leave her daughter with this man was surely evidence of her lies?

You will want to make sure that you have talked to someone about your own experiences so that this does not unduly influence you in the way you talk to your children. The other difficulty is if you have no experience whatsoever of the issue. If you have never known anyone who has been abused (given the statistics, the chances are you have, but they haven't told you they've been abused), you might hold the belief that abuse only happens to 'other people'. We know from large population studies that sexual abuse occurs in every social stratum in society. If you believe otherwise then you need to inform yourself about the issue – believing that it could never happen to my child is leaving your child at risk. Being open to the possibility that your child could be sexually abused will help you take the initiative in protecting your child better. We don't know enough about how children are protected from sexual abuse so I think the safest benchmark to go by is: sexual abuse can happen to anyone.

Due to the nature of sexual abuse and the serious consequences of uncovering such abuse, it is a difficult topic to discuss with family or friends when you have a concern, particularly if you are unsure and afraid of getting it wrong. You may be reluctant to rely on your usual confidantes as they may know the person concerned. You may feel paralysed. Don't carry this alone. Find someone to share your concern with. If there is no one in your family or social network that you can trust, use the range of helplines available.

Sometimes parents feel deskilled when faced with questions from their children about sex and sexual abuse. Or they may observe their child playing with their private parts and not know how to respond. They may react impulsively in a negative way and admonish the child, later regretting it. Sometimes parents will observe children engaged in sexual play with each other and feel perplexed as to how to respond to this behaviour. It's almost as though all their knowledge and skills about parenting goes out the window; they feel out of their depth when it comes to dealing with sexual behaviour. There are some good online resources to inform parents about what is regarded as appropriate sexual play among young children and what is regarded as sexually harmful behaviour (see www.cari.ie).[15] When dealing with the latter, parents need to address this the way they would address any other harmful behaviours they see their child engage in – they need to stop it, teach their child it is not appropriate and monitor the child closely to make sure it doesn't happen again.

Know Your Child

I have heard parents speak about their child by saying: oh she'll be safe. No one would dare touch her. She'd tell immediately when referring to an assertive, outgoing young girl. While it is true that people who abuse children are more likely to target the quiet child who may be less likely to tell anyone, this is not universal. Children can be vulnerable to abuse for many complex reasons.

---

15 McGrath, K. *Understanding and Managing Sexualised Behaviour in Children and Adolescents: Guidelines for Parents and Carers* (Dublin: The CARI Foundation, 2010).

The danger with the attitude captured above is that if this child was abused and didn't tell for some time, perhaps they wouldn't be believed when they finally did. I have met children in this situation. Because they didn't tell immediately, they felt that their parents wouldn't believe them and so this made it more difficult for them to tell.

Knowing how your child might respond to something like sexual abuse will help you consider possible strategies that you can teach them about telling you if something happens. It is always a good idea to give a little more than what they are looking for. This way you can gradually increase their knowledge about the topic in a way that will not overwhelm them. People talk about 'age appropriate' conversations. This can be confusing for parents who are not sure what 'age appropriate' means. My advice is to think about your own child – what do *you* think is appropriate for them? What do they know already? How can you build on that so they do not feel overwhelmed or just switch off and take very little in? If you know your child, you will know how to pitch the conversation.

How you talk with your child about these sensitive and potentially embarrassing topics is important. Children typically find it difficult to talk to their parents about all things sexual. While on balance both younger boys and girls find it easier to talk to their mothers than their fathers, Irish research[16] has found that boys are more inclined to talk to their fathers and girls more inclined to talk to their mothers. It is worrying to note that a survey conducted in 2010 by researchers at the Royal College of Surgeons showed that fewer parents surveyed in 2010 were talking to their children about sexual matters than parents surveyed in 2003.

Knowing your child is crucial in terms of how you go about this. You will need to proactively seek opportunities to have these conversations. You will need to 'test the waters' with your children and if they find the conversation intolerable, you will need to ease

16 See http://epubs.rcsi.ie/cgi/viewcontent.cgi?article=1053&context=psycholrep

off and try again another time. You may even need to be firm and insist that this is an important conversation to have. Even if they don't engage in a discussion with you, it's important that you take the opportunity to tell them how important it is that they come to you if they have a worry like this.

If you have more than one child, it can be a good idea to talk to children together. It's a good idea to find out what they know already so that you can 'fill in the gaps' as a starting point. It's also a good idea to use television, radio programmes or newspaper articles on the topic to prompt a conversation. This can be done in a casual way but it gives the clear message that you are open to having these conversations, and that it is important to do so. As our children's social world grows, we as parents know less and less about what their daily lives entail. We can't always be there to inform them and guide them. It's therefore best to get in early with these conversations. Don't wait until something happens in the naïve belief that 'it's too early'. It's never too early to protect your children.

Listen

The key signs that a child is being sexually abused are in many ways no different from the signs that something else is wrong in a child's life. Noticing changes of behaviour and commenting on these changes can give your child an opportunity to tell you if there is something on his mind.

When talking about child sexual abuse with a child who is very young, it is best to be guided by them. Try to use language that they use. You will have taught them words for their private parts. Use these words to explain that these are very private and special parts of the body and no one else should see or touch these parts except Mammy or Daddy or whoever cares for the child. Young children are accustomed to having their nappy changed or being bathed and this is a good time to explain this to children. Teaching children that it is only okay for others to touch their private parts when they are cleaning them or helping them when they are sore is a good start to protecting them from sexual abuse. As previously mentioned, sometimes younger children find it difficult to tell someone they have been abused because they don't understand what is happening, they don't realise it is wrong, or they don't have the words to describe their experience. Young children might say things like: Daddy hurt my pee pee. This could mean that when Daddy was changing his daughter's nappy and saw that she had nappy rash, he rubbed some cream that hurt his daughter as he applied it. It could also mean that Daddy has problems managing sexual urges to abuse his daughter and this statement is the only way this little girl has of telling someone that something terribly wrong is going on.

When children ask questions, this is a good opportunity to have a conversation about sexual abuse. Having conversations from an early age about the possibility of child sexual abuse can pave the way for a child to bring this up at a later age if they have questions about what is going on in their lives. Don't leave it too late. Children will find out for themselves without their parents telling them and the information they get may not be too reliable. There is a funny cartoon I saw recently showing a parent sitting on a chair facing his son, who is playing on a computer. The Dad says: let's talk about sex. The son responds with a knowing smile: sure Dad, what do you want to know?

If you have begun these kinds of conversations with your children when they are young, it is easier to revisit them when your children develop into teenagers. There is research to suggest that regardless of what age a child is when they are abused, they are more likely to disclose this abuse during their teenage years. Adolescents are caught in a difficult bind when trying to tell someone about abuse they have experienced. They understand that it is wrong. They understand that the person who abused them will get into trouble. They often don't want others to know about what has happened to them, as they may fear that they will be judged in some way or seen as 'damaged goods'. These fears are not unrealistic. Many young people are judged and receive very negative attention when others find out they have been abused. Families do fall apart following a disclosure. Many young people also understand that their parents will be terribly upset by such revelations. They often want to protect their parents from this knowledge, preferring to bear the burden alone. However, they also often feel under a lot of pressure to tell. They may be feeling the psychological impact not only of the abuse experience but also the burden of keeping the secret. Young people I have spoken to describe it as a 'pressure cooker': both wanting and not wanting to tell.

Teenagers who are drinking alcohol are particularly vulnerable to abuse by peers. It is also extremely difficult for these young people to tell their parents. Often, they will be afraid that they will get into trouble – perhaps they have been drinking, staying out later than they were supposed to, or went somewhere they shouldn't have gone. They will often feel that they are in some way to blame for what happened, that they somehow should have been able to stop it, no matter how unreasonable this belief is. Research has shown that young people are quite good at predicting how their parents will react when they disclose experiences of sexual abuse. Children who predicted that their parents would not believe them were right – their parents didn't believe them.

Ask

With younger children, it's a good idea to use stories with animals or cartoon characters to teach about sexual abuse. The Council of Europe, as part of their child abuse prevention campaign, published a lovely little book for use with children under the age of five. It tells the story of a little puppy who is abused by his uncle (see www.coe.int/oneinfive) It deals with the issue of sexual abuse in a very sensitive way and makes it easier for parents to have these kinds of conversations with their children.

There is a lovely YouTube clip that I came across several years ago that I use in my classes. It is an animation from Islamabad with English subtitles[17] Basically, it shows a young boy and girl in the playground sharing with other children what their Mum and Dad told them that day. Their parents had sat them down for a chat and told them that children are their own best friends and this is why they take such good care of themselves – brushing their teeth, washing their hands, brushing their hair and eating healthy food, and taking care that no one harms them. They make sure that when people touch them, it makes them feel good, not bad. The parents describe good touches as those that make us feel good from the heart. Bad touches hurt us and make us feel bad and angry from the heart. The children demonstrate some good touches to their friends (a hug), and bad touches (a pinch on the cheek). Then the parents described another kind of touch: a secret touch. This is when someone touches them in a secret way and may ask the child not to tell anyone about it. The parents emphasise that anyone can use this kind of touch – any grown-up or an older child. The parents explain to their children that a secret touch can make a child feel embarrassed or ashamed or angry or scared from the inside. They also explain that children often feel that something is wrong when they are touched in this way. The parents insist that it is never the child's fault when this happens. The parents also describe how people who give secret touches often appear to love children very much but sometimes they may scare them or threaten them. The person may also try to pretend that the secret touch is a game. The parents rehearse with their children what to do – to run away, to shout, to ask for help and most importantly to tell their Mum and Dad. The children make up a song about this and sing it together in the park. They finish off their lesson to their friends by asking all the children to tell someone else about this lesson.

17 The video can be found at http://www.youtube.com/watch?v=oo_PUSb8GrY

This is a good resource for parents and it covers a lot of the features that as a parent you would like to cover in a conversation of this nature with your child. It's worth mentioning though that many people who abuse children do not ask the child to remain silent. The child knows not to speak of it. Often they don't need to be told this. Also, sometimes people abuse children in such a way that it makes the child feel 'good'. A child who is feeling lonely or sad may welcome the attention they receive from the person who goes on to abuse them. The person who abuses them may be very nice to them and may have developed the relationship with the child over time, a process we call grooming. It's hard for the child to tell early on in the process because the behaviour is so subtle. By the time the child clearly recognises the behaviour as abuse, they may feel that they have in some way gone along with it by not telling someone earlier. The child then is caught in a bind. If I tell will people not wonder why I didn't tell earlier? Will they believe me? Will they think it's my fault? Also, most children are abused by someone they know, someone in their immediate family or their extended family or someone close to the family. Younger children in particular are more likely to be abused by a family member or someone close to the family as these are the people with access to younger children. This is a delicate issue to raise with children – that someone close to them, maybe even someone they love, can touch them in this way. Finally, it's important to understand that sexual abuse extends beyond touching, although this is the most common form. If a child is raped, they may not think of this as a 'touch'. Also, exposing children to sexually explicit material either by showing them pornography, videos, or forcing them to witness adults or older children engaging in sexual behaviour are all forms of child sexual abuse.

An interesting finding from studies examining children's experiences of telling someone that they have been abused is that very often this was preceded by a parent or interested other asking the child questions. Questions such as: is something bothering you lately as you seem in bad form? Why do you not want Mary to babysit? You used to love going to Granny's – what's wrong?

It is a difficult topic for a child to bring up. They probably feel very uncomfortable about what happened. They may understand quite well that talking about this will create major trouble and they won't want to be the ones to be the cause of it. They may feel ashamed and guilty for 'allowing it to happen' and may fear that they will be blamed. They may need help in telling us; asking them questions can be just the kind of help they need. One teenage girl described to me how she thought her mother would guess what was going on: I even said to my Mum part of the reason I didn't tell her was because I was waiting for her to guess: I was waiting for her to say to me, 'has this happened?'

Older children and teenagers are quite likely to confide in a friend before they tell a parent if they have been sexually abused. Nurturing a relationship with your children's friends and making sure they see you as approachable can encourage them to come to you if they are worried. While you obviously need to be careful not to intrude on the boundaries of your children's friendships, talking to their friends and asking them their views on sensitive issues can help to establish and maintain good channels of communication.

Reassure

In this context, reassurance can take the form of providing accurate and reliable information, or providing emotional support when your child does come and talk to you about their worries. Firstly, teaching your child about their rights is important. The United Nations Convention on the Rights of the Child (UNCRC) has outlined a series of children's rights that various governments all over the world have signed up to in the spirit of recognising the dignity of children. The Convention itself and a child-friendly leaflet are available on www.dcya.gov.ie.

As previously noted, being informed certainly helps young people to deal with difficult situations. While teenagers on average do talk more to their friends, they still turn to their parents first and foremost for information and emotional support.

Children often test the waters to see if it is safe to speak out. What fears are they likely to have about telling? Do they think they would get into trouble? If so, you can reassure them that this is not the case, that when someone does this, they are responsible and totally to blame. Are they afraid of someone else finding out? This is trickier to deal with as it is inevitable that other people will find out. Don't make promises that you won't be able to keep, such as I promise I won't tell anyone. Even when children ask for the secret to be kept, they can feel relieved when this responsibility is taken from them. The statutory services that are responsible for child protection will need to be informed if there is a concern in relation to sexual abuse. If the person who has behaved inappropriately is a family member, other family members will need to be informed so that other children are protected and the person concerned can get help. The important message to keep reinforcing is that the person did something wrong, not your child. One of the unfortunate impacts of sexual abuse is that the child feels responsible, they feel ashamed or dirty and therefore don't want anyone else to know about it.

While it is good to ask children questions, be careful about 'putting words in your child's mouth'. Parents can often finish sentences for their children or otherwise fill in the gaps that children leave in their communications. Given the gravity of discovering abuse it is essential that both accurate and reliable information is obtained from children when they begin to tell of their experiences. There may be legal proceedings, during which the story of when, how and why the child first spoke out will come under scrutiny. While we want to show our children that we are interested in hearing more about what they have to say, the best way for parents to approach this situation is to keep their questioning to what we call 'open questions' so that we don't provide the answer within the question. We don't say did he touch you? Instead we might say what happened? In this way, we are trying to keep the conversation as open as possible and reduce the likelihood that we will misunderstand or misinterpret what the child is trying to tell us. Both children and adults are vulnerable to suggestive questioning. Encouraging children to give us information without asking closed questions (questions that require just a yes or no answer) will give us more reliable information about what the child needs to tell us.

If your child does say something that suggests that he or she has been sexually abused, be careful how you react in the immediate moment. You may be feeling shocked, horrified, incredulous, disgusted. However, you want to encourage your child to tell you more. Children in this situation will be very sensitive to your reactions. They may have worried and brooded on this for weeks, months, even years. You will want them to experience you as supportive, first and foremost. Children who have been sexually abused are more likely to tell if they get a supportive response from their parents and they are also more likely to fare better psychologically if they have supportive parents. You will want them to know that you are there for them and that you will always be there for them, no matter what they tell you.

Don't assume that you know what it's like for your child: you must feel awful. That must be very frightening for you. It may be that if the same thing happened to you, you might well feel this way. It may be that your child has these feelings, but be open to the possibility that their feelings may be very different to what you imagine. Every child is unique and every child's experience is unique. It might be better to check in first with them before you make assumptions. Questions like: and what is that like for you now? or were you frightened? might be a better option for some children. Don't assume that your child has been traumatised.

It's important to take comfort from the fact that while many children suffer considerable distress following an experience of sexual abuse, many others are able to cope with this experience and with the proper support, many children are able to move on with their lives and not suffer unduly as a result of the abuse. How a child is impacted by the experience of abuse depends on many factors, including the nature of the experience itself, but also how psychologically robust the child is, what personal resources they have and what supports they have from the people around them. Children who are able to recognise abuse for what it is and seek help early tend to do better. Children who have parents who are supportive of them but not too distressed themselves also do better.

One father I spoke with about what it was like when his daughter told him she had been sexually abused, described his own reaction: with me it was the end of the world, the whole world has caved in on me ... it was the worst thing that ever happened and it killed me, really really ate me up ... for the first eight months I thought this was the worst thing that ever happened, nothing worse could ever happen now. This father attended a parents' support group and couldn't believe how differently he felt a year later, having received support and reassurance from other parents and professionals. When I spoke with his daughter, she was coping very well. Part of what made it so difficult for her to speak out was that she knew her parents loved her very much and that this would be a nightmare for them if they found out what was happening. The closeness she enjoyed with both her parents actually got in the way of her being able to tell them what was happening. So, while we want to keep our relationships with our children loving and strong, we also want them to feel that whatever they tell us, we will be able to manage it, we will not get so upset that they will feel it is the end of our world.

One of the reasons I have found working in this area so rewarding is that I have met so many children and adults who, despite the painful experiences they have had in their lives, are able to move on and lead fulfilling, enriched lives. Witnessing the transformation that takes place when children and adults 'recover' from the trauma of sexual abuse reminds me of how powerful we are as human beings and how much we can change our lives with help and support from others. No one can ever erase what happens to us in life, but we can come to make sense of what happened and how we feel about it in ways that help us cope and get on with our lives.

Remember ...

* **Know Yourself:** Be aware of your own difficulty in being open to the possibility that your child could be abused. Talk to others about your own feelings about sexual abuse and how you can talk with your child about this possibility.

* **Know Your Child:** Reflect on your child's strengths – what would protect her from being abused? How is she likely to react if someone approaches her in this way? How might she communicate this to you? How can you help her come to you if something happens to her?

* **Listen:** Watch out for signs that all is not right in their world – changes in behaviour, emotional upset. Children often show signs of wanting to communicate something before they can verbalise it.

* **Ask:** Create opportunities for conversations to happen. How was today? You look a bit down, are you okay? Disclosure often occurs in the context of being asked about general psychological well-being.

* **Reassure:** If your child does tell you about something that concerns you, reassure him that they are right to tell you, that this behaviour is never the child's fault. Tell him there are professionals who deal with these issues and they will help make sure it doesn't happen again.

Talking with Friends

This chapter is a little different from the others in this book because it focuses on children communicating with other children. The reason I think it is worth devoting a whole chapter to this is because as children get older, they confide more and more in their friends. When they are young, a parent is typically the first person that children turn to with their worries. A parent is the first person they tell when something bad happens to them. However, teenagers are more inclined to first confide in a friend before telling an adult. If we can equip our children with the skills to both confide in others when they are in need and be able to respond to their friends' needs when they are on the receiving end of shared confidences, they will be better able to cope with these situations as they emerge. Of course, as parents we would prefer if our children come to us in the first instance with their worries and anxieties. This is not always possible for children. They may be afraid of our reaction. They may worry that we will be angry or annoyed with them if they need to tell us about something bad that has happened. They may already feel that they are to blame for this, and so they may fear that we too will blame them. They may be worried that we will be upset. They may not want us to worry about them. They may be afraid of what will happen if they tell us something that we will need to act on. Young people, depending on their age, will have many fears and concerns about the consequences of telling us about their problems. The older they are, the more sophisticated their thinking is about the possible consequences of telling. Younger children are very astute in being able to sense when we are upset. They are very good judges of how we will react. Older children will weigh up the pros and cons of telling; they may decide that, on balance, it is best to stay quiet. They too are very good at judging our potential reactions to what they tell us. If they do decide not to confide in us in the first instance, we will want them to be able to turn to someone they can tell. It may be their friends, or it may be another adult that they can confide in. In either case, we will want them to be able to talk to someone.

Part of our job as parents is to help our children learn how to engage in relationships with others in their lives. Children's relationships with their parents is what we call the primary relationship. For most children it is the first relationship. It is therefore very important in that it lays down the template or plan for how our children develop relationships with others throughout life. In the past few decades there has been a growing appreciation of the importance of sibling relationships. Many children spend a lot more time with their siblings than they do with their parents and this experience has a powerful impact on them – for good or bad. How children negotiate relationships with siblings is just as important for them as their relationship with their parents when the time comes to form friendships with their peers. In the home, we can help our children navigate the territory a little easier than we can when they are forming friendships with peers in school or the local community.

As children get older they will spend more and more time with their friends. They will want to be more like their friends, dress the same, like the same music, engage in the same fun activities. Being part of a group – thus the 'same' as the others – becomes more important. They need to learn how to stand up for themselves in such relationships, how to both give and receive, how to cope when things go wrong, to understand when it's okay to be different from the others. They will need help with these developmental tasks in the early years and as they get older they will need to be supported in different ways. They still need help, but the kind of help they need varies from child to child, and from one stage of life to another. As children enter the teenage years, they will often be more influenced by their peers than they were when they were younger. They will care more about what their friends think. As I have said, they will often turn to their friends with their questions and their worries before they discuss these with their parents. It is not that they need their parents any less, but the way in which they need them differs. The kind of support that they wanted as younger children is different from the kind of support they need and want as teenagers.

Know Yourself

I have already talked about how our own experiences of childhood and our experiences of being parented influence how we are as parents. In helping our children deal with other relationships, it is a good idea to reflect on how this was for us as children. How did we get on with our brothers or sisters? Where were we in the family – youngest, middle, oldest? How did this impact on how we got along with our siblings? How did we settle a row? Were we an only child? What was this like? Did we have many friends? What kind of children were we drawn to? Did we like those who were like us or were different from us? How did we cope when things went wrong in our friendships?

And how are we now? Do we have a lot of friends or a few close friends? Do we value friendship? Do we make an effort to maintain our friendships? Do we confide in our friends? Do we talk things through as part of the process of reflecting on the decisions we need to make in our lives? Do we bottle things up? Would our friends know what is going on in our lives if they were asked? We all differ in terms of how much we share with our friends, how much we talk to others. The value that we place on these relationships, however, will influence the value that we place on our child's friendships.

It may be that we struggled with friendships when we were young, that we looked to other popular children with envy. It may be that we would wish for our children that same popularity that we saw other children enjoy, appreciating the benefits, both social and emotional, that popularity with peers brings for children. We may undervalue the qualities that we did have as children. If we were quiet, with few friends, we may place too much value on being sociable and gregarious. It is the meaning of friendships that is important for children, not the number of friends. Having few friends who are highly valued and supportive is of much more benefit than having a large group of friends where the relationships are 'diluted' and don't foster the same level of closeness and support.

When our children are younger we have so much more say in who they have as their friends. Typically, these are the children of our friends or neighbours. We have a lot of opportunities to monitor their peer interactions and a lot of opportunities to intervene when we see fit. As is natural, we can be very defensive when it comes to how other children interact with our children in ways that we don't like. Our own wounds from friendships past can be reopened and we can find ourselves judging other children according to their behaviour. We can find ourselves reacting to even very young children, assuming intent where none was present. We can think that a child hit out at our child deliberately because we observed the sequence of events. But we can assume too much. We can lose a sense of perspective and appreciation of how it is to be a young child. We can 'put into their minds' the motivation of an older child or an adult because the behaviour looks the same. But often the child concerned is simply acting impulsively. They are not persistently out to get your child or to undermine him or to make her look stupid. In this way, observing children's interactions can remind us of difficult experiences we have had and we can misinterpret what we see. Having difficult experiences with peers affects how we interpret social cues; we are more likely to judge an interaction more negatively than someone else observing the same interaction who doesn't have a history of difficult peer relationships.

As our children get older their horizons widen and they get the opportunity to exercise more choice about whom they spend time with. We may not always agree with their choice of friends – we may find it hard to understand why they are attracted to certain children more than others. We may want them to be more friendly with certain children because we like those children or because we like their parents. As part of encouraging their independence it is important that we allow them the freedom to explore this arena, to make their own decisions, and to learn from these experiences. This can be challenging at times. As adults, we are better able to anticipate the consequences of certain situations. However, we have to learn when to speak and when to stay silent. Young children are not able to see these consequences in the same way that we are. Explaining them does not help them see them any better. It is often through making their own mistakes that they learn.

Know Your Child

From an early age your child will show their personality through how they interact with other children their own age. Their temperament will show firstly in the way they play with you and then when they play with other children – one child may prefer to play alone while another child may always want someone else to play with. While it is good for children to be able to mix with others and to form friendships, it is also important that children are able to develop their own personalities and not be pressurised into being a certain way if this is not right for them. In getting to know your child and what fits for him or her, you will be able to reflect on how you can support their growth and help them develop their own communication patterns with their friends.

Knowing what upsets or delights your child will help you manage their play interactions and foster opportunities for them to enjoy playing with their friends. If you know that your child doesn't like it when their friend engages in physical play, you will need to intervene and minimise the opportunities for this to happen. By doing this you are demonstrating to your child: if you don't like when she constantly pushes you, you need to sit further away from her when you play together. You will need to teach your child how to communicate this in a way that doesn't push friends away: please don't push me. That hurts. If you notice when a particular combination of children are playing football together that the competition is so fierce that your child is not enjoying the game, you might intervene by suggesting another game or reorganise the 'teams' to dilute the competition a little. In these simple ways, you are showing your child how they can manipulate their environment to make life more pleasurable and enjoyable when spending time with friends. You are also showing them that sometimes it is important to communicate clearly what you like and that sometimes it is better to communicate this in a different way – through your behaviour rather than through words. As each child will differ in terms of what they enjoy doing, this can require some negotiation when you are trying to manage a number of children playing together. The important lesson is that each child is different; they enjoy different games and different ways of playing those games. Validating each child's right to be themselves helps them develop a sense of their own likes and dislikes and their entitlement to have particular preferences. They are then in a better position to be able to compromise: I don't like playing football but I'll play a game with you now if you play cards with me afterwards.

When children are in school, parents generally get a good idea from teachers about how their child socialises with others in their class and school. While a parent will know their own child well and how they function in the home and local environment, the teacher is well placed to comment on how the child is developing when compared to other children their age. Knowing how your child plays in the schoolyard can tell you a lot about their personality and their social development. Do they prefer to seek a quiet place to sit and play alone? Are they in the middle of games? Do they tend to play with just one other child? Who are the children that your child is drawn to? What is it about them that draws your child to them?

When your child experiences conflict in their friendships, you want them to be able to turn to you for support. You can help them to reflect on their friendships by offering them feedback based on your knowledge of them: it seems to me that you really like Sarah. You seem to enjoy spending time with her. By doing so, you help them to reflect on and know themselves better, know what they value in friendship, know what makes them uncomfortable, and what makes them feel devalued in their relationships with friends. Having a good sense of this for themselves will help them to be assertive in relationships, to expect to be treated well by their friends and to treat their friends in the way they expect to be treated themselves. How your child deals with conflict in their peer relationships will lay the foundations for good friendships. Being able to say things when they need to be said without getting too angry or too upset is a challenge for us all when we need to say something difficult to a friend. However, we are not honouring the friendship if we don't trust our friends enough to be able to be honest with them. Helping our children to develop the skills of communicating with their friends when they feel hurt or annoyed, while at the same time respecting their friends' point of view, is an important part of their social development.

As children get older they may become more secretive about when things don't go so well in their peer group. They may be reluctant to bring it up and may need encouragement to be able to talk about what's happening. They may be afraid that you will interfere in some way – that you will try to be the referee that you were when they were younger. They will need reassurance that they can talk to you about their worries without your stepping in to fix them. Talking out loud about what's bothering them can help them make sense of it themselves. It can help them find their own solutions.

Listen

Listening to your child when they are in the company of other children will give you a good insight into their world. Watching them play with other children, listening to their conversations with their friends and listening to other parents and their observations about your child will give you much needed information about how to help your child communicate when they are with other children.

As mentioned previously, many parents have gathered invaluable information about their children by eavesdropping on conversations between them and their friends. Driving the car, listening to the children chatting in the back, oblivious to your presence, can provide a great opportunity to hear about the little spats that took place in the schoolyard that day or how a certain child in the class is always getting into trouble for hitting other children, or how a teacher may be struggling with managing particular children in a class. Hearing your child talk with her friends about how social situations are managed in school, their views on the fairness or otherwise of how they were managed, can give you a good sense of your child's social development. Hearing how your child talks to his or her friends will tell you something about their relationship. How much is said and how much isn't said? Listening to how their friends talk to them may also give you some insight into how they perceive your child is in a way that may not be obvious to you through either observing your child in play with others or from speaking with your child about his friends.

Watch your child when she is playing with her friends. Watch the way they take turns talking or playing. What is the pattern? Does one child dominate the other? Is one more vocal than the other? Do they each take turns like a seesaw, first one then the other, in an easy rhythm? See how the children's personalities are displayed through the way they play together. See how different they are and in what ways they are alike. How do they manage each interaction? Do they complement each other? Do they constantly clash? Or is it a little bit of both? Which combinations of playmates work well and which don't? And in what contexts – which games? Which houses? The same pair of children may get on great if they are playing ball together but struggle to get along if they are doing a jigsaw together. When children are younger, parents are often in the role of referee. They need an adult nearby to mediate – to step in if things get out of hand. They are learning to deal with conflict. As they get older they will need to learn to do this for themselves. Some children are natural referees – they take on the role of mediator in their group of friends.

Given the extent to which children use the internet and online social media sites, it is also important that parents not only keep up to date with how children are communicating with each other, but also monitor these communications in whatever way they can. While children can be very adept at using online communication, they are understandably less well informed about the potential risks of such usage and how to manage them. They need parents to help them manage these risks, just as they do in real-life social situations. There is much good advice for parents, based on research across Europe, on how parents can support their children's use of the internet (see www.eukidsonline.net). Informing ourselves about security settings, managing and sharing personal information, and encouraging our children to come to us if they are exposed to inappropriate images on the internet have become the new challenges faced by parents in the twenty-first century. While parents need to encourage children to explore the opportunities available online we also need to pay attention to and monitor our children's online engagement, while respecting children's privacy needs.

As previously mentioned, it's a good idea to keep in contact with friends' parents. This is easier to do with younger children. As our children get older it takes more effort as there are fewer opportunities available to us to see these parents on a regular basis. Keeping channels of communication open between parents enables us to share our concerns, learn from each other, and hear about what is happening in our children's lives. Some children will become more private as they get older, sharing less about their daily activities. Others will be more talkative. If parents pool their resources, there is a better chance that everyone can benefit. Some young people will be more inclined to chat to their friends' parents than to their own. It's important not to interpret this as a personal affront – it can be easier for them to speak to someone who isn't part of their daily lives. Talking with other parents and making it clear to our teenage children that we do keep in touch with other parents often serves as a strong protective factor in helping our children (and us!) navigate their way through life. It helps us to know what's going on in their lives and therefore how best to support them.

Ask

By showing an interest in your child's friends you are also showing an interest in them. It sends the message that you value your child's social network and that you care. You appreciate that their friends are important to them and you respect their right to choose their own friends.

When your child is younger, your way of 'asking' is through observing what is happening and checking this out with your child. You can notice who they like and who they don't appear to like. You can get an idea of why this is. As your child gets older, you can use these opportunities to encourage them to talk to you about their interactions with their peers. Having conversations about friendships can help your child reflect on these relationships. It can help them be more aware of what it is they like about their friends and what it is they value in these friendships. It can also provide opportunities for conversations when their friends have experiences that they have not had, for example, if a friend has a nasty experience with another child in school. This can create an opportunity to talk about your child's view on this: who was in the wrong? Was it dealt with fairly? How did her friend feel about it? What did she do to console her friend? What would it be like if this happened to her?

You may notice when your child doesn't appear to be playing with children they used to play with. Commenting on this can encourage your child to talk about it. They may not have particularly noticed this change – in which case, it may reassure you that it doesn't reflect any 'falling out' between your child and his friends. Or it may be something that your child is trying to make sense of himself and he might benefit from talking it through.

More and more, children communicate with each other through social media and play with each other through online gaming platforms. If parents make a point of encouraging their children to talk about these experiences, it is easier to know what's happening and to be there if your child experiences something that upsets them. Being present in the room where they play their online games may provide opportunities to get a sense of the kind of communication that is happening during these games.

Children will inevitably come into contact with unpleasant images on the internet. It is important that they can talk to you about this. They may be reluctant to bring it up – they may be afraid that you will curtail their internet use if you know what material they are exposed to. They may feel guilty about viewing such material and be afraid that you will blame them for 'accessing' such sites and not understand fully how the internet works. Initiating conversations about these topics is a good idea. This conversation can lead to discussing how to limit this exposure, and how to manage access to the internet in such a way that your child is better protected from such intrusive images and materials.

Parents can sometimes find it a struggle to balance the privacy needs of their children with their own need to know what is going on in their children's lives. While we want to encourage them to create their own social network and look to their friends for fun and for support, we also want to make sure that they stay safe. Of course it is important not to be too intrusive, to allow our children the freedom to explore their relationships without too much interference from us as parents. A good question to ask is: if I don't know how can I protect? Being informed about what is going on in our children's lives as they interact with their peers helps us know when to ask questions and when to stay quiet. Checking in with ourselves – do I need to know this? And if so, why? – might help us decide whether asking our children questions about their social activities is coming from a place of protection or just plain nosiness!

Finally, keeping in contact with our children's friends is also a good way to encourage open communication. It may be that our son or daughter is really bothered about something and has told their friend but hasn't been able to tell us. It may be that their friend feels it is really important that we know about it. If we are perceived by our children's friends as approachable, they will be more likely to share information about our children with us.

Reassure

While it is important to be honest and authentic with your child it is also important to hold back when you don't like their friends. It may be that you don't like the way that your child is being treated by his or her friend. In this instance, it is better to focus on the behaviour rather than on the friend or the friendship. You can still like a person and not like their behaviour. This is less threatening for your child to listen to. They may not feel the need to defend their friend quite so much if the focus is on the behaviour rather than the person. Another idea is to help your child from an early age to use 'I' statements when they are having a difficult conversation with a friend. An example would be, instead of saying: you really hurt me when you did that, you might say: I felt really hurt when you did that. In this way, you are not blaming the other person but you are pointing out that something happened that you felt hurt about. A classic example is: you made me angry rather than: I feel angry about what you said. It can be argued that no one else can make you feel a certain way. They cannot force you to feel angry; rather, you are the one with the control over your feelings. However, their behaviour can contribute to how you feel. It is much more effective communication to simply state how you feel rather than focusing on what they did.

Children who feel good about themselves, and have high self-esteem, expect others to treat them well. Children who feel poorly about themselves and have low self-esteem don't expect much from others. If we can engender in our children a sense of self-worth and self-esteem, this will hopefully create an expectation on their part that they will be treated well in relationships. They will expect people to treat them well. Being able to recognise when your friends are not being good to you is a really important part of the process of forming nurturing friendships. For so many people, tolerating bad behaviour from friends stems from a low sense of self-esteem. If we can teach our children that they do deserve better, this can help protect them from forming relationships where they are not treated well.

Remember ...

* **Know Yourself**: Be a good role model and value your own friendships; show your children how you can talk with your friends and get support with your daily struggles and in so doing teach your child the value of friendships and peer support.

* **Know Your Child**: Help your child understand what they value in a friend and to choose their friends according to these values. Encourage them to share their thoughts with their friends.

* **Listen**: Watch your children as they play with their friends; be there for your children when they come to you with their worries and conflicts about peer relationships, and help them to learn how best to deal with these. Keep in contact with their friends' parents so that you can pool your resources and collect information about your children's lives.

* **Ask**: Take an interest in your children's friends and ask them about their friends and their friendships. Get to know more about their online activities and encourage them to talk to you about this.

* **Reassure**: Be a friendly advisor to your children to help them navigate the territory of friendships. Teach them the social skills needed to maintain friendships.

EIGHT

When Professional Help is Needed

Love is blind. An age-old saying that has many different meanings. The most common interpretation is that loving someone blinds you to their faults. It can also blind parents to the possibility that all may not be right in their child's world. The wish and indeed need for our child to be happy can blind us to their sadness. We can mistakenly find reasons for why they are a bit down today, or why they are different from other children. It is their uniqueness that we love after all, their individuality, the little characteristics that mark them out from the crowd. Some parents, in response to the question who is she like? will answer proudly, she's like herself. So when does 'unique' become 'strange'? When does 'needs space' become 'needs help'?

The main focus throughout this book has been on how we and our children communicate with each other. We know that helping our children talk about what is going on in their lives is good for them in terms of developing their identity and their emotional well-being. We also know that by keeping the communication channels open with them, they will be more likely to come to us and talk with us if there is something troubling them. In this chapter, I am going to talk about how we can talk with our children when we are worried there is something wrong. Anxiety and depression are the two most common mental health difficulties experienced by people all over the world. This goes for children as well as for adults. And while it is difficult for parents to recognise the early signs of anxiety and depression, it is even harder for children and young people to recognise what's going on. It is unusual for a young person to come to a parent and say: I think I'm depressed. They are much more likely to complain of being tired all the time, of not sleeping well, of losing their appetite or finding themselves 'comfort eating', of being bored or fed up, or of avoiding activities that they used to enjoy, such as spending time with friends.

Many parents struggle with facing up to the fact that their children need help. They feel they should be able to do this by themselves, that in some way they have failed if they find themselves in the situation of needing to ask for professional help. But sometimes we need to learn other ways of loving our children. And sometimes our love isn't enough. We can follow all the 'best' advice and it simply isn't enough. For some of us and for some of our children, daily life is a real challenge. Dealing with the everyday ups and downs that other people seem to be able to take in their stride is an uphill struggle.

Knowing When Help Is Needed

As we discussed in earlier chapters, younger children often communicate their distress through their behaviour or through psychosomatic complaints – headaches, tummy aches and nausea. These are normal manifestations of distress. It is when they persist over a period of time or begin to interfere with daily functioning that we need to think about whether they are indicative of something more serious. It is up to parents to notice these changes in behaviour or persistence of complaints and to monitor whether these are just passing difficulties. Children of different ages have a tendency to experience different kinds of worries and fears. For example, preschool children may be afraid of the dark. Some children are afraid of the toilet – something comes out of their body and then disappears down the loo to a lot of noise and swirling of water. This can be upsetting, but is what we regard as a developmentally 'normal' fear to experience. The childhood fear of the 'bogeyman' or the 'monster' in the bedroom at night is universally experienced by children of a certain age and passes as the child matures. Children of various ages can be afraid of something happening to their parents – I've mentioned earlier how this can manifest itself as a school phobia. The child is afraid to go to school because they are worried that something bad will happen at home. Those in the 'middle-childhood' years may experience a preoccupation with death and may be particularly anxious about dying themselves or of someone close to them dying. With the self-consciousness that comes with adolescence, there can be a fear of standing out from the crowd, of being made a fool of, of being exposed.

It is when these so-called-normal fears and anxieties become overwhelming and get in the way of the child's daily life that we need to be more concerned and wonder if this is a symptom of serious underlying difficulties. Children with mental health issues typically find it hard to cover up their difficulties in the school setting, so teachers can be an important source of information when parents notice changes in their child's mood or behaviour. Children may find it difficult to concentrate in class when they are worried or feeling anxious; they may withdraw into themselves and interact less with their playmates. They may be more impulsive and get into trouble in school or they may find themselves in conflict with their peers in the schoolyard. It may be that they are struggling academically and this is the source of their emotional distress – that they can't keep up in class and are not able to ask for help. Some children may throw themselves into their school work as a way of avoiding difficult feelings, withdrawing from their social activities by saying they want to study for exams when they are really feeling quite down in themselves; studying is an excuse to avoid being in social situations where they feel anxious.

Teenagers may use drugs such as alcohol or cannabis as ways to relax, to escape from the demands of daily life. In a way this is self-medicating – using substances to alter one's mood in order to avoid dealing with real-life difficulties. It can also be difficult to know what's causing what: is the low mood a result of excessive use of alcohol or cannabis? or: Is the growing dependency on these drugs a way of coping with difficult feelings?

Over the past twenty years there has been a growing awareness that many serious difficulties such as autism and schizophrenia can be seen on a spectrum or continuum with other difficulties that share similar features but do not impact on daily life to the same extent. Rather than thinking in terms of a person 'having' a condition, we can think in terms of a person exhibiting certain features that may or may not be at the level or intensity that requires professional help. One example of this may be the child who has a very rich fantasy world and who may prefer to spend time 'daydreaming' than interacting with others. When does this idiosyncrasy become a problem? Some useful questions to ask of yourself may be: is it interfering with my child's daily life? If so, in what ways? Is it getting in the way of him paying attention in class and so impacting on his learning? Is she struggling with friendships as a result of this tendency to focus so much on her inner world? Is my child struggling with differentiating between what is real and what is fantasy?

Some difficulties are detectable from an early age. Developmental difficulties such as those reflected in Autistic Spectrum Disorders (ASD) can be identified before a child starts school. Others such as Attention Deficit Disorder (ADD) or Attention Deficit and Hyperactivity Disorder (ADHD) will become more evident during the primary school years as children are met with the challenges of an educational system that requires them to learn and behave in certain ways that they will find particularly difficult. Eating disorders such as anorexia nervosa and bulimia typically arise during the teenage or early adult years, as do psychotic difficulties such as schizophrenia, although in unusual cases younger children can develop these difficulties. If parents are concerned about their child having a particular kind of difficulty, information is very accessible on the internet. However, it is good to know where to look, as there is also much information available that may be unreliable. Government agencies, voluntary organisations or professional bodies tend to have helpful information that is prepared by professionals and based on established research or reputable publications. Examples of these are www.headstrong.ie or www.youngminds.org.uk. It may also be a good idea to consult your GP or, if possible, arrange to speak with a child psychotherapist or child psychologist.

It can be extremely distressing for parents who are trying to help their son or daughter manage these difficulties without professional help. The helplessness they feel watching their son or daughter deteriorate before their eyes can be overwhelming and can get in the way of parents being able to ask for help.

Talking with children about mental health difficulties is challenging. When children are suffering in this way, they are often less likely to talk with you as this is part of their problem: being unable to express themselves. It can be very difficult to describe the feelings they are having; they may be reluctant to say the words out loud as this can make it more real and they may be fearful of the consequences of letting their parents know the thoughts and feelings they are having. They may be wondering are they going 'mad' and be fearful that if they talk about it, others will believe that they are 'mad'. Parents too may be reluctant to confront the issue. If they speak about it with their child, they can no longer avoid the reality that something is wrong and that help is needed. Parents can cling onto the hope that it is a passing phase and that their son or daughter will 'come right' if they just wait it out.

Because many young people with mental health difficulties have a particularly negative or distorted way of thinking about their problems, this can make it harder to engage them in conversation about what's going on and about the possibility of seeking help.

Whether this negative thinking style is a result of the mental health problem or is partly a cause of it is a little confusing. We know that people who suffer from depression have a distinctly negative 'thinking' style that compromises their ability to pull themselves out of their depressive mood by themselves. We also know that children with a negative outlook on life are more likely to develop difficulties like depression later in life. Either way the reality is that when young people are having difficulties it is harder for them to talk about themselves than when they are well.

It may be that your son or daughter is angry a lot of the time and this makes it difficult to create an opportunity to have conversations that focus on their well-being. This anger may in some cases be their way of communicating their distress that things are not okay in their world. It can feel very hurtful if all your attempts at conversation are dismissed. Your questions about their well-being may be rebuffed with a grunt or a shrug and it is hard to keep trying when you are being treated in this way. One tip that sometimes works for parents is to stand back and imagine yourself in their shoes. Imagine if you were grumpy all the time, biting the head off anyone who spoke to you or grunting at them when they tried to engage with you. How must you be feeling if this is the way you are behaving? Not very happy or content with life I imagine. Empathising with your son or daughter in this way might help offset your frustration or irritation a little, enough to help you persevere and think up other ways of reaching out to them. It may be that rather than asking them how their day went you could make some suggestions based on what you do know: I guess it's been a long day. You look tired. For some young people, this might be too direct, too much focus on them. A comment on how they look can aggravate them further. In this case you might just say: I guess it's been a long day. Don't think that just because they don't respond, they are not hearing you. Young people need to have their feelings validated, especially when they are not able to talk about them. Sometimes you have to do the talking for them, just like when they were babies and they didn't have the words to express themselves. Back then, they used their body language to communicate their distress through crying, reaching out, pushing away. And you were left to interpret these behaviours yourself. Now they are also using their body language – the avoidance of eye contact, the stooped shoulders, the 'going to the bedroom' routine, the monosyllabic responses to your questions. It is up to you to try to understand what's going on for them and find opportunities to name their feelings in as unobtrusive a manner as you possibly can.

It is not unusual in families for parents to have different views about what's going on with their children and how to respond to them. One parent may feel the other parent is overindulgent. One may feel the other is too strict and hard on the young person. A parent may feel that their son just needs to be told to get on with their life while their partner may be concerned that their son's 'difficult' behaviour is a reflection of something more serious. I've often found that this difference of opinion can be a strength for couples rather than a difficulty, particularly if there is mutual respect in the relationship and each values the other's opinion. It can help them explore the range of possible explanations for their daughter's mood swings or their son's withdrawal, testing out these ideas in different ways and together planning a time frame of when and how to seek help if there is no improvement over time. It's important where there are differences of opinion that parents talk to each other as much as possible, each listening to the other and trying to see things from the other person's point of view. Keeping an open mind will help you notice the things you need to watch out for in your child.

You may find it particularly difficult to talk with your child about your concerns if you yourself suffer from mental health difficulties. You may be terrified that they are beginning to show signs of developing the same problems that you have struggled with for years. You may feel that it is your fault that they are now having these difficulties. Many serious mental health difficulties have been shown to have a strong genetic component: that having parents with depression or anxiety issues increases your child's risk of developing such difficulties.

The relationship between genes and mental health difficulties is complex but we do know that we can change how our genetic makeup impacts on our risk status: protective factors such as stable supportive family relationships, good levels of education, and supportive peer relationships can offset this risk. You can use your experiences to help your child cope: what worked well for you? What helps and what doesn't help? Some of this may be useful for your child, some of it may not but you can use your experience for good rather than let it get in the way of being the parent you want to be.

Getting Help

If having considered the various possibilities, you feel that it is necessary to seek help, having a conversation with your child about this is the first step. Some parents will bring their child along to a doctor, a psychologist or psychotherapist and ask them to have a word with them, not having informed their child of why they are going to see this stranger. The child is left wondering what on earth is going on and it makes it more difficult for the professional to get to the bottom of the concerns. It's important not to label the child as having a problem unless your son or daughter names it in this way. An alternative can be to simply state that you are worried about them, stating why you are worried, and drawing on examples of their behaviour that have concerned you. You can be clear that you are the one who is concerned and you are the one who feels it is necessary to seek help. As a parent you can say that you are struggling with figuring out how to help your son or daughter and you feel that it would help to talk to someone about it. This can open up a conversation about the issue in a way that is not identifying your child as being or having the problem but rather that you as a family need some help. Most children who are struggling to cope will welcome this. It can be a great relief to them when a decision is made to seek help. They can feel heard and understood, even if their parent isn't able to solve the problem for them.

Generally speaking, mental health difficulties develop over time. So it takes time for people to get back on their feet. And it usually happens by taking baby steps – one small step at a time. For parents trying to help their son or daughter on the road to recovery, it's the little things that matter. The small gestures of warmth, the few kind words of comfort. It's about being proactive and finding opportunities to say these words of encouragement or praise – finding something good that happens, paying attention to it, commenting on it. For the young person, there may be a lot of negativity in their day. As a parent, you need to try to rebalance the negative with some positive. And it can be difficult to find those opportunities when you're worried sick yourself and may even be feeling some of the despair that your child feels. Nevertheless, your child needs you to be the one to be strong and creative, and to shed some positive light into their life on a daily basis. It may be an upbeat comment about what you're going to do today, showing a positive attitude. It may be asking your son to bring in some coal for the fire and thanking him. It may be asking your daughter to go to the shop for a last-minute errand. Thank them. Show them your appreciation. Say what a great help it is – these little things that make a difference to all our lives. There is a lot of research on volunteering, why people volunteer and give of their time to help others. One of the findings from this body of research is that helping others is a protective factor against developing mental health difficulties. Helping others makes us feel good. Young people who are struggling with their own psychological difficulties may find it difficult to access opportunities to help others. As their parents, we can help them find these opportunities by asking them to do things for us or for others. They may need a bit of a push in this direction.

When young people are feeling down, they will have less energy and less motivation to do things that in themselves help them to feel better. You may feel inclined to think that because they have very little energy, it isn't fair to ask them to do things for you. It's important to understand that the more physical activity you can engage them in, the more likely it is their mood will lift. Sometimes you have to insist. It will help.

Our physical health and our mental health are intertwined. If we are not looking after our psychological well-being, our physical health will suffer. Similarly, if we don't look after ourselves physically, our mental health will suffer. Physical activity is extremely important for young people's psychological well-being. Many young people who develop mental health difficulties describe having given up sports in the months or years prior to developing difficulties. Involvement in sport can be a protective factor for children in maintaining good mental health. The basic routines of eating, sleeping and some form of physical activity are important to maintain, and generally require immediate attention as a first step on the path to recovery from mental health difficulties. Teenagers in particular can develop poor eating habits, late night TV viewing or computer gaming routines that interfere with their sleep pattern, resulting in less exposure to sunlight and reduced physical activity. Getting these basic routines re-established can require a firm hand on the part of parents, but it is a necessary one.

If you have decided that professional help is necessary, it's important to do some research. Unfortunately, despite government strategies over the years highlighting the importance of equal access to services for all, there is quite a difference in service availability depending on where you live. A local GP might be a good option. You can discuss what services are available, both public and private, in your area. Social work departments involved in working with families on a daily basis tend to have good comprehensive information about psychology, counselling and psychotherapy services. With younger children, public health nurses generally have a good idea of what's available. Voluntary organisations, because of their dependence on public funding, will advertise their services either through posters or websites and generally give a good description of the range of services they have available. Local libraries are also a good source of information about local services. Schools are generally well informed of relevant services available in the locality. At secondary level, guidance counsellors may be available in the schools as either a consultation point or as someone who can offer your child individual support.

THERAPEUTIC APPROACHES

Whether you choose to attend a psychologist, a psychiatrist, a counsellor, or a psychotherapist, they will typically work from what we call a particular theoretical perspective. The main approaches to counselling and psychotherapy are referred to as behaviour therapy, cognitive behavioural therapy (CBT), person-centred therapy (PCT), systemic family therapy, and psychoanalysis or psychodynamic psychotherapy.

Behaviour therapy helps the family to understand what is **triggering certain behaviours** and what the child is getting out of this behaviour. The therapist will help the parents to learn how to modify the child's behaviour and how to teach their child more adaptive ways of coping.

There are lots of effective ways of helping young people and their families to behave in a different way so that everyone can function better. The belief is that the maladaptive behaviour is causing the distress. If we change the behaviour, we alleviate the distress.

Cognitive Behavioural Therapy (CBT) focuses on the child's **thinking**, how this thinking influences behaviour and feelings.

There are well-developed strategies for changing the way we think about ourselves and others that can help us think differently about the world. This change of thinking style can change our mood. A more positive attitude and thinking style can thus help lift our mood and help us feel better.

The belief is that distorted thinking patterns and false assumptions about ourselves and the world around us is causing the distress. If we change the way we think, we can change the way we feel.

Person-centred therapy (PCT) focuses on creating **the right environment** for the child to feel listened to and heard, to feel authenticity in our interactions with others, and to feel unconditionally loved.

This type of therapy is less about 'doing' and more about 'being'. The focus is on providing the young person with a positive experience of a relationship with another person in the belief that this will help the young person discover what it is they need to do and how to do it. There is an emphasis on the child's sense of agency and the therapist's belief in the child – that they have within them the solutions to their difficulties and the purpose of therapy is to help them find those solutions.

The belief is that we all have within us the ability to realise our potential but the reason we have not been able to do this is because we are not met in our lives with the attitudes of empathy, congruence and unconditional positive regard. Many of our problems stem from the absence of the right conditions to help us grow.

Family therapy focuses on viewing the child's difficulties in the context of **how the family functions** as a whole.

The family therapist works with the whole system, in this case the family. Whether the therapist sees the family or sees the individual child, they hold this perspective in mind when working therapeutically.

The belief is that when we develop difficulties, even though it may seem to be something within us, there are aspects of the family system that are contributing to our difficulties and aspects that can help us overcome those difficulties.

Psychoanalysis or psychodynamic psychotherapy focuses on **bringing into conscious awareness** those **unconscious drives and wishes** that influence our way of being in the world.

The psychodynamic therapist will help the child to make sense of their difficulties, through play or through talking, to access his or her unconscious thoughts, fears and anxieties. The pursuit of insight is important – making sense of ourselves and of the world.

The belief is that psychological difficulties are a sign that we have unconscious fears or wishes that are impacting on our daily lives in a way that is unhelpful and that need to be brought into the open or into consciousness and understood.

How counselling or psychotherapy works will vary. Play is used a lot in therapy, particularly with younger children, as this is the way younger children often communicate what's going on for them. It can be difficult to put their experiences into words. Children find it easier to enact stories and pictures that reflect their feelings and experiences. Storytelling is another method that is used. Through stories about other children, feelings and themes can be named that may apply to this individual child and that can be a 'way in' for children to begin to explore their own experiences. Fairy tales work in this way in the home – reading fairy tales to children from a young age can help them to make sense of the sometimes intense feelings that they may have difficulty in processing.

Children sometimes like to draw or to use other materials such as clay to create images that depict their innermost thoughts and feelings. Drama is another medium that is used sometimes with children – creating a stage for them to act out their stories.

While toys are typically used with younger children, older children and adolescents also sometimes like to work with drawing, painting, clay, or simply talking. Sometimes workbooks are used to help the older child or teenager to focus – they provide a structure to discuss difficult topics. Children and young people may be seen individually, in groups or as part of family sessions. This can depend on resources and what's available, and also on what is right for the young person at a point in time.

Typically, when a child or young person attends therapy, parents will also be expected to attend regular appointments. This is in recognition of the important role that parents play in helping their children to manage life. For most children, families manage without the help of professionals. For those who do need additional help, the difficulties have typically escalated to a level where both the parents and the young person have exhausted their own personal resources and need help to get back on track. Parent support at this point is just as important as support for the child or young person. Groups can also be very helpful for both young people and parents as there is the opportunity to see that they are not alone. They can also learn tips on how other people with similar difficulties have managed.

Remember ...

✳ **Know Yourself:** Reflect on your own expectations of your child and your expectations of yourself. Is this more than you can cope with? Do you have enough support to get by? Are you reluctant to ask for help?

✳ **Know Your Child:** How long have you been concerned about your child? What have you tried? Is there any improvement? Is it time to seek additional help?

✳ **Listen:** What is your child trying to communicate? Watch out for the changes in routine or mood levels. Is this a sign of psychological distress, a passing phase or simply their personality?

✳ **Ask:** Try to put words on your child's feelings for them if you feel they are having difficulty expressing themselves.

✳ **Reassure:** Reassure your child that together you can get help and that things will get better.

Afterword

I hope you have enjoyed reading this book as much as I have enjoyed writing it. I hope it has helped you to think about yourself and your child in a way that is familiar to you as well as opening up new possibilities for you in the way you talk with your child. We are always learning, always wanting to know more, to understand better, to be better parents. But it's also important to stop and reflect on all we do know, all we do understand. Sometimes what we really need is reassurance that we're doing okay. We don't always need answers elsewhere – sometimes it's best to look to ourselves and what we already know about ourselves and about our children and use that knowledge to guide us as parents. You know your own child best. You have a lot of the answers, so as well as seeking new knowledge and advice on how you can do things better, you need to listen to yourself and consolidate what you already know. And of course, it's good to talk about it!